Ryan Thomson
The Eczema Deception

Contents

2

3

Copyright Page
THE ECZEMA DECEPTION
By Ryan Thomson

For more information, visit:

Website: www.theeczemadeception.com

Email: theeczemadeception@gmail.com

HEALING
HAPPENS!!!

"2014"   "2024"

DISCLAIMER

This book is based on m observations, and rese: Withdrawal (TSW), the 1 pharmaceutical industry. **I am not a ~~doctor~~, pharmacist, or medical professional, and nothing in this book should be interpreted as medical advice.**

The content of this book is intended for **informational and awareness purposes only** and reflects **personal opinions** rather than universally accepted medical conclusions. **Readers should always consult a licensed healthcare provider before making any medical decisions.**

This book includes **commentary, criticism, and personal viewpoints** regarding medical training, pharmaceutical practices, and the healthcare system. These views are **expressions of personal opinion and should not be interpreted as statements of absolute fact.**

The author believes in **freedom of expression and open discussion regarding patient experiences**, particularly concerning the medical treatment of eczema, steroid dependency, and Topical Steroid Withdrawal (TSW). **However, the author makes no claims of conspiracy, malicious intent, or unlawful behaviour by medical professionals, pharmaceutical companies, or healthcare institutions.**

Statements regarding the **medical field, pharmaceutical industry, or healthcare system** are made in **good faith**, based on the author's personal journey and publicly available research. They are **not**

intended to harm, defame, or mislead, but rather to encourage discussion and awareness of patient experiences.

Legal Release of Liability

- The author and publisher **do not provide medical advice and are not responsible for individual health outcomes.**
- The reader agrees that any **medical decisions, treatment choices, or lifestyle changes** should be made in **consultation with a qualified healthcare provider.**
- The author and publisher assume **no responsibility for errors, omissions, or possible consequences** resulting from the use of the information in this book.
- Any **mention of medications, treatments, or alternative approaches** is for **informational purposes only** and **should not** be taken as a directive to follow or discontinue any treatment.

Final Notice

By reading this book, you acknowledge and agree that.

- The content is **opinion-based**, not professional medical guidance.
- The author **is not liable** for any medical or legal decisions based on this book.
- The book **does not accuse any individual, company, or profession of illegal activity** but

rather presents **personal opinions and experiences.**

- Any **claims made about the pharmaceutical industry or medical system are personal interpretations and not verified factual claims.**

If you have a medical condition, always consult a licensed healthcare provider before making changes to your treatment.

THE ECZEMA DECEPTION

My Journey To Recovery From Topical Steroid Withdrawal (TSW)

Introduction: The Hidden Epidemic of Topical Steroid Withdrawal (TSW)

"For years, I trusted my doctor's prescriptions. At first, they helped, until they didn't. Until my skin betrayed me. Until my skin rebelled, flaring worse than ever. Until the very treatment meant to heal me became the thing that destroyed me."

This is Topical Steroid Withdrawal (TSW), a condition so severe it turns everyday life into a waking nightmare. My skin burned, itched relentlessly, and shed like a body at war with itself. Sleep became impossible.

The worst part? Most doctors still deny its existence.

The Day Everything Changed

I thought I had eczema. That's what the doctors told me. That's what I believed, until the day I stumbled across a video that changed my life.

At that point, I had spent years trapped in a cycle of worsening symptoms. The stronger the steroid, the worse my skin became. My hands and feet were unrecognisable, red, raw, swollen, blistered, and cracked to the point where even the simplest tasks felt impossible. Walking

16

was agony. Work became unbearable. Life as I knew it was slipping through my fingers.

And no doctor had answers.

I saw doctor after doctor. Prescription after prescription.

And continued to get worse.

I had lost myself in the process.

Then one night, lying awake in agony, scrolling through desperate online searches, I found it.

A video.

A dermatologist in America, speaking about something I had never heard of before.

Topical Steroid Withdrawal.

I sat up, my breath catching in my throat.

As the doctor described the symptoms, I felt a chill run through my body. It was as if he was speaking directly to me, describing every single thing I had been going through for years. The burning. The flares. The oozing. The skin that seemed to get worse the longer I used steroids.

Everything clicked.

For the first time, I had an answer. A name for what was happening to me.

And with that answer came a horrifying realisation.

The very medication I had been prescribed, the creams I had trusted, the treatments I had followed to the letter, they weren't healing me. They were destroying me.

A Battle for the Truth

I wish I could say that, after finding that video, everything got better. That I took action and healed overnight.

But the truth is, that was only the beginning.

17

Because when I confronted my doctors with this information, they dismissed it.

They told me Topical Steroid Withdrawal (TSW) wasn't real. They told me I was making it worse by stopping treatment. They told me I needed more steroids.

I was gaslit, ignored, and abandoned by the very system I trusted.

But I had seen the truth.

And once you know the truth, you can't unsee it.

Why This Book Exists

This book isn't just my story, it's a warning and a guide.

I was never supposed to go through this. I never had eczema before steroids. I was a healthy, active man, living a full life.

Until one small prescription set off a chain reaction that would rob me of everything. My health. My confidence. My ability to work, to sleep, to function.

No one warned me. No one told me the truth. By the time I realised, it was too late.

I had to find it myself, too late, after years of unnecessary suffering.

I don't want that to happen to you.

That's why, alongside sharing my journey, I also share the lessons I learned the hard way. The things I should have tried sooner. The treatments and changes that made a difference. The strategies that could help ease the pain, speed up recovery, and offer even the smallest relief.

I'm not a doctor, and I don't have all the answers, but I know what it feels like to be lost, desperate, and searching for hope.

If you're going through this now, know that you are not alone. If you've never heard of Topical Steroid

Withdrawal (TSW), this might just save you from experiencing it. And if you're a doctor, I beg you, start listening.

Because this shouldn't be happening. And it's time the world started paying attention.

CHAPTER 1. THE BEGINNING OF IT ALL

Chapter 1:01. About Me

My name is Ryan Thomson, born in 1978 in Canterbury, Kent, a city steeped in history, known for its cobblestone streets, medieval architecture, and the towering Canterbury Cathedral, a landmark that has stood for centuries.

Canterbury wasn't just a city to me, it was home. It was where I grew up, where my family lived, and where I built my life. The chiming bells of the Cathedral, the bustling high street with its mix of old-world charm and modern shops, the familiar faces on a stroll through Dane John Gardens, all of it formed the backdrop of my everyday life.

This is my Topical Steroid Withdrawal (TSW) story, but it's also the story of how a seemingly minor decision, a simple doctor's visit, set off a chain reaction that would derail everything I had worked for.

1:02. A Life Without Skin Problems

Before that fateful day, I never gave my skin a second thought.

I never struggled with acne.

I never had unexplained rashes or dryness.

I never dealt with irritation, flaking, or redness.

From my teenage years into adulthood, my skin was flawless, something I had taken for granted. While others battled spots, struggled with oily skin, or experimented with different face washes and treatments, I did nothing. A quick wash in the morning, maybe some aftershave if I could be bothered, and that was it. Simple. Easy. Forgettable.

That's the thing about good health; you don't appreciate it until it's gone.

By this point in my life, I had been married for nine years and had just welcomed my third child into the world.

Life was busy.

Life was good.

Life was full.

I worked as an electrician, specialising in price work, a system where the more you completed, the more you earned. I thrived in it.

I was fast, efficient, and well-organised.

I knew how to get jobs done to a high standard without wasting time.

I had mastered shortcuts and techniques that maximised productivity and earnings.

It wasn't just about money, it was about providing stability for my family.

With my wife managing the home and the kids, I took full responsibility for bringing in the income. There was no room for setbacks, no space for anything that could slow me down.

You push through. You keep going. That's just how life worked.

But then came the day that changed everything.

1:03. The Spot That Started It All

A tiny, annoying red spot on my arm, no bigger than a mosquito bite. It itched, but not enough to be a concern. I ignored it at first, assuming it would clear up on its own.

But a week went by, and it was still there.

Not spreading.

Not painful. Just, lingering.

No one likes unexplained things happening to their body, even minor ones. It plays on your mind, the what-ifs, the curiosity, the nagging feeling that maybe you should just get it checked out.

So, not thinking much of it, I did what anyone would do, I made an appointment with my GP.

The doctor's visit was fast, too fast.

I sat down, rolled up my sleeve, and before I had even finished explaining, the doctor was already glancing at my arm with barely a flicker of interest.

No real questions.

No curiosity about what could have caused it.

No discussion about lifestyle, work, stress, or any other factors that might have played a role.

Just a quick look, a vague mutter, "Just a little inflammation."

That was it.

And before I could even process what he had said, he was scribbling out a prescription with muscle memory, like this was just another routine transaction, another nameless patient with a forgettable issue.

In and out in under five minutes.

I barely had time to ask anything before he was handing me a slip of paper and sending me on my way.

1:04. The First Tube of Hydrocortisone

The prescription was for hydrocortisone cream, a mild topical steroid.

At that moment, I didn't think twice about it.

A steroid? So what?

The doctor prescribed it, so it must be fine, right?

It's just a cream. A little tube of white ointment. Nothing serious.

With zero concerns, I picked up the prescription from the chemist, took it home, and started using it exactly as instructed.

It seemed harmless.

I was confident that in a few days, this would be gone,

and I'd move on like nothing had happened.
Except, nothing changed.

I was two weeks in now, and still nothing had changed.
The red patch remained, unfazed, unmoved, as if the cream did nothing at all.
I had no reason to panic, not yet, at least.
Instead, I did what anyone would do when a treatment isn't working,
I went back to the GP.
"I rolled up my sleeve, expecting questions. Instead, before I could finish explaining, the doctor had already scribbled out another prescription.
Without hesitation, the doctor handed me a stronger steroid. No discussion, no questions, just another tube, another prescription.
The cream was called Betamethasone Butyrate, a medium-potency steroid, one level stronger than hydrocortisone."
"At the time, I didn't know what that meant. To me, it was just another tube of cream. Another 'solution.' Another harmless-sounding name on a prescription slip."
"But Betamethasone Butyrate wasn't mild. It was more aggressive, designed to suppress inflammation deeper within the skin. Stronger steroids meant faster results, or so I thought."
"I picked up the prescription, went home, and started using it exactly as directed. Twice daily. Thin layers.
"And this time? The red patch actually started to fade."
"For the first time in weeks, I thought I was getting better."
"I had no idea that, beneath the surface, the damage was

only just beginning."

What I didn't know, what the doctor never mentioned, was that my skin had already started to change. The mild steroid hadn't worked, and now I was on a stronger one.

But why did I need something stronger?

Why hadn't my skin simply healed?
I had unknowingly stepped into a trap that would soon consume my life.

Photo 1 "This was me before it all started, clear skin, no clue what was coming."

Photo 2 "A year into steroids, only my hands affected at this point"

CHAPTER 2. GOING DOWNHILL

Chapter 2:01. The Slippery Slope

For a while, life carried on as normal.

I was still working, still providing for my family, still doing everything I had always done.

I was still applying the cream, just like the GP told me to.

I didn't question anything.

Why would I?

The betamethasone seemed to work, at least, that's what I thought.

The red patch would improve, sometimes, it looked almost completely gone.

Then, a few days later, it would come back, angrier, redder, itching more than before.

But the GP had told me to keep using the cream, so I did.

Morning, and night, it became part of my daily routine.

I wasn't worried.

I wasn't questioning anything.

I wasn't thinking about steroids, addiction, or long-term effects.

It was just a tube of cream, something that was meant to help me.

2:02. The Routine That Became a Habit

At first, I applied it casually, whenever I remembered.
Then, it became a habit.
Wake up, apply the cream.
Before bed, apply the cream.
It was no different from brushing my teeth, just another thing to do to keep my body in check.
The instructions from the doctor were clear,
"Use a thin layer, twice a day."
I didn't see it as overuse. I saw it as following the doctor's advice, and making sure the treatment was doing its job.
And for a while, it felt like it was working. Until it wasn't.

2:03. The First Signs of Something Bigger

It was around eight weeks in when I started noticing something, off.
At first, it was just little things.
The spot wasn't healing fully, it would look fine one day, then flare up the next.
I would go longer without using the cream, thinking it was healed, and it would return worse than before.
It wasn't just one spot anymore, I was noticing similar patches on other areas of my arm.
That's odd,
Still, I wasn't panicking.

28

Maybe it's just stubborn?
Maybe I need to be more consistent?
So, I kept applying the cream.
But then, something new happened, and it was
something I couldn't ignore.

2:04. The Blisters: A Warning I Didn't Understand

It started with just a few.
Tiny, clear blisters, barely noticeable at first.
Three or four scattered across my palms.
Small, harmless-looking, like little bubbles trapped
beneath my skin.
No pain, just an itch.
But this itch was different.
At first, I ignored it, just another minor irritation.
I'd dealt with itchy bites before, and little annoyances.
But this was something else.
This wasn't an itch you could scratch away.
This was deeper, almost internal, like something
crawling under my skin, screaming for relief.
It was maddening.
No amount of scratching helped.
No amount of rubbing made it stop.
It was just there, constant, relentless, and unshakable.
At night, it got worse.
I'd lay in bed, rubbing my hands against my sheets,
against the wooden frame of the bed, against anything

that might ease the sensation.
But the more I scratched, the more irritated my skin became.
And the blisters? They weren't going away.
Instead, more started appearing.
One day, I counted them.
There were at least ten now.
Scattered across my palms, creeping toward my fingers.
This wasn't normal.
I told myself it was just eczema, that maybe I had developed some kind of allergy.
But deep down, something felt off.
So I went back to the GP.

2:05. "Just Common Eczema"

I sat in the stiff-backed chair of the GP's office, hands outstretched, palms up, showing him exactly what I was dealing with.
I had expected concern, maybe even a proper examination.
At first, he barely reacted. A quick glance, a slight nod, as if this was nothing more than a routine rash.
But then, something changed. He leaned in just a little closer this time, his eyes narrowing as he examined the cracks and blisters across my palms. He pressed against the skin lightly, watching how it reacted.
Still, there were no tests. No deeper questions.
Then, just like before, he reached for his prescription pad.

"This is just common eczema."

Eczema?

I frowned. I had never had eczema in my life.

I had gone 32 years with flawless skin, not a single sign of any chronic skin condition.

How could I suddenly develop eczema now?

I hesitated for a second, but I didn't push back.

He was the doctor.

He knew best. Right?

And who was I to argue?

I nodded, still looking down at my hands, the blisters glistening beneath the overhead light. Maybe I was overthinking it?

Maybe it really was just eczema?

But something deep inside me, some gut feeling, was telling me that this was more than just eczema.

2:06. A Dangerous Upgrade: The "New and Improved" Prescription

The doctor sighed and looked at his prescription pad, tapping the pen against it for a moment.

"This should help," he said.

I glanced up, expecting to see the same cream I had been using before.

But instead?

He was writing out a stronger steroid.

Betamethasone Valerate 0.1%, also known as Betnovate.
I later learned that Betnovate is a potent topical steroid,
significantly stronger than the ones I had been using
before. It was another step up the steroid ladder.

Mild steroids - Hydrocortisone.
Moderate steroids - Betamethasone Butyrate.
Potent steroids - Betamethasone Valerate (Betnovate).

I was now at a level three steroid, a potent drug that
should have come with serious caution.
But once again?
No warning about addiction.
No discussion about side effects.
No mention that my skin was already dependent on
steroids.
I walked out of there with the prescription in hand,
convincing myself this was progress. That maybe this
time, it would actually work.
But deep down?
I wasn't so sure.

2:07. The Blister Cycle Begins

I left the GP's office feeling like I should trust him, but
at the same time, something didn't sit right.
How could I suddenly have eczema after 32 years of
clear skin?
Why didn't he ask about my medical history?
Shouldn't we be looking for the cause, not just treating

the symptoms?

But I shoved those thoughts aside and did exactly what I was told.

Morning, and night, I followed the routine religiously. Steroid cream first, rubbed into my hands in thin layers. Doublebase moisturiser next, sealing in the treatment.

If the GP wasn't worried, why should I be? I assumed I'd wake up one day and my hands would be back to normal.

But that day never came.

Instead of healing, my hands began developing a pattern, a cycle that I would soon become trapped in.

It started subtly at first. A few tiny, clear blisters beneath the skin. Nothing alarming. Just a little itchier than before.

But then, the cycle took hold, a cycle I would come to know all too well:

Step 1: Small clear blisters appear beneath the skin. At first, there would only be a few, tiny pockets of fluid deep under my skin. They looked harmless, but the sensation they brought was anything but.

Step 2: The itch intensifies, deep, relentless, impossible to satisfy. This was far from a normal itch.

Step 3: The blisters burst, dry out, and my skin cracks. After a few days, the blisters would rise to the surface, pop, and then dry out completely. It should have been a relief, but instead, my skin turned dry, brittle, and cracked open in places. The deep fissures made every movement painful.

Step 4: I ease off the steroids. Since my hands were looking better, I assumed I didn't need the cream anymore. I wasn't one to use medication unless I had to. The blisters had disappeared. My hands weren't perfect, but they weren't as bad as before. So I backed off.

Step 5: Within days, the blisters return, worse than before. And then, almost like clockwork, the cycle would start again.

More blisters. More itching. More discomfort.
And this time? It was worse than before. Like my skin had become even more sensitive, even more reactive. And so, I reached for the steroid cream again. I followed the instructions again. And the cycle continued.

2:08. Was This Eczema? Or Something Else?

I didn't realise it at the time, but what I was experiencing had a name: pompholyx eczema, also known as dyshidrotic eczema.
Pompholyx is a type of eczema that affects the hands and feet, causing intense itching and deep-seated blisters. It typically flares up in cycles, exactly what was happening to me.
Triggers include stress, heat, allergens, and irritants like chemicals or even moisture.

But here's the thing,
I had never had eczema before. And I had no known allergies, no history of skin problems. So why now? Why out of nowhere?

Something didn't add up.

And what I didn't know then, what no one told me, was that topical steroids can actually cause and worsen pompholyx. They might suppress the symptoms temporarily, but they don't fix the problem. And for some people, they make the skin dependent on them, leading to withdrawal reactions that look identical to eczema itself.

But I didn't know that yet.

All I knew was that I was trapped. The worst part? I hadn't even realised it yet.

2:09. The Job, the Itch, and the Frustration

At this stage, it wasn't ruining my life, not yet. But it was starting to affect my work.

The Problem with Gloves

As an electrician, wearing protective gloves was mandatory, part of my PPE. But I quickly noticed something:

Heat triggered the itch.

The moment my hands started sweating inside those gloves, the itch ramped up to unbearable levels.

I couldn't focus. I'd constantly have to pull my gloves off, not because I wanted to, but because the burning, crawling sensation was too much.

At first, I tried subtle ways to relieve it:
Rubbing my hands against my trousers when no one was looking. Clenching and unclenching my fists, trying to distract myself. Scratching when I could, making sure no one noticed.

But the more I scratched, the worse it got. And the worse it got, the slower I worked.

2:10. The Price of Slowing Down

I wasn't on a salary, I was on price work.
The faster I worked, the more I earned. The more I earned, the better I could provide for my family. Every wasted minute meant lost money.

But now? I was losing minutes every day to this maddening itch.

At first, I'd stay 15 minutes late to make up for lost time. Then 30 minutes. Then an hour.

I was working longer, just to compensate for something I didn't even understand.

And when I got home? I was tired. Irritable. Short-tempered.

At home, it wasn't causing major problems yet, but I was definitely moaning about it. I must've annoyed my wife and kids with my constant complaints, but the truth was. It was getting worse.

2:11. The Point of No Return

I was trapped in a cycle I didn't understand.
At work, I struggled to keep up.
At home, my wife started noticing my frustration more and more.
The itch was relentless.
The flares were coming faster, what used to take weeks was now happening in days.
And for the first time, I felt real fear.
"Why is this getting worse, not better?"
"Why does my skin only improve when I'm using steroids?"
"Am I going to be stuck with this for life?"
I didn't realise it then, but I had already crossed into dangerous territory, the point where my body was fully dependent on steroids, where stopping them would become a living nightmare.
But at this stage?
I still trusted my doctor.
I still believed I was just unlucky.
I had no idea I was on the road to full-blown withdrawal.
That road had already been paved. I just hadn't reached the end of it yet.
Looking Back: Was I Just Another Victim of the System?
Hindsight is a cruel teacher.
Now, looking back, I know I was already addicted to topical steroids, I just didn't recognise it. And that's the most dangerous part. Steroid addiction doesn't feel like

addiction.

There's no high.

No obvious warning sign.

No moment where you realise, I'm hooked.

You just keep applying the cream, because that's what your doctor told you to do.

And so, like millions of others, I unknowingly became a casualty of a medical system that hands out prescriptions without ever questioning why.

2:12. A Medical System Built on Band-Aids, Not Solutions

Doctors don't look for causes, they look for quick fixes. And steroids? They're the easiest fix of all. Rash? Topical steroids. Itchy skin? Topical steroids. Eczema? More topical steroids. No one ever asks why. No one ever tells you what happens when you stop

Steroids are handed out like harmless moisturisers. Patients are told to use them liberally, daily, sometimes for years. But what they're never told is this:

The longer you use them, the more dependent your skin becomes.

Over time, your body stops producing its own cortisol because it's getting a synthetic version from the cream. And the moment you stop? Your body panics.

The skin flares worse than ever.

The burning, peeling, and nerve pain begin.

Your body screams for more steroids.

So, you keep applying them, believing you need them.

The cruel irony?

It's not the eczema that keeps getting worse, it's the steroids themselves.

2:13. Are Doctors to Blame? Or Are They Just Uninformed?

I've wrestled with this question for years.

Did my GP fail me? Absolutely.

Did he intentionally harm me? Probably not.

But here's the reality, doctors are supposed to be the experts.

I wasn't the one with medical training. He was.

I trusted him. I followed his advice.

Yet, not once did he stop to ask:

"Why has this man, who has never had skin issues before, suddenly developed a severe, persistent condition?"

Instead of investigating the root cause, he blindly escalated my treatment, more steroids, higher potency, without ever considering that the treatment itself could be making me worse.

The truth is, doctors aren't taught about Topical Steroid Withdrawal (TSW).

They aren't taught about the dangers of long-term steroid use.

They aren't taught about alternative treatments or natural

healing methods.

Why?

Because their education, their textbooks, and even their treatment guidelines are heavily influenced by pharmaceutical companies.

Pharmaceutical companies don't exist to heal people.

They exist to make money.

The global dermatology market is worth billions.

The topical steroid industry alone is projected to reach $8.5 billion by 2027.

Big Pharma's entire business model thrives on lifelong customers.

Think about it.

If they cure people, they lose customers.

But if they keep people dependent on medication, the money never stops flowing.

That's why the most profitable drugs aren't the ones that heal people.

They're the ones that create lifelong dependence.

Insulin for diabetics.

Antidepressants for mental health.

Opioids for pain.

Steroids for eczema and skin conditions.

These drugs don't cure, they just suppress symptoms.

And the moment you stop taking them? Your body spirals into crisis.

That's not medicine.

That's a business model.

And I?

I was just another pawn in their billion-dollar empire.

2:14. The Steroid Trap: How Many People Are Stuck in It?

At first, I thought I was the exception. Then I realised I was part of an epidemic. Thousands of people, just like me, had followed the same path, small rash, steroid prescription, temporary relief, worsening flares. The only difference? Most of them still didn't know the truth.

This is how steroid addiction begins.

And yet,

Dermatologists ignore it.

Doctors deny it.

Big Pharma profits from it.

But for the people stuck in it? It's hell.

So Who Is to Blame?

I've thought about this a lot.

Is it Big Pharma?

Yes. They knowingly create drugs that don't cure, only manage. They profit off suffering.

Is it GPs and dermatologists?

Partly. Many are undereducated, blindly following what they're told. But that doesn't excuse their lack of critical thinking.

Is it patients?

Not at all.

We trust our doctors to do what's best for us.

We follow medical advice because we assume they know better.

But the reality?

Most doctors are just middlemen for the pharmaceutical

41

industry.

They aren't researchers.

They aren't pharmacologists.

They aren't dermatology specialists.

They read guidelines, prescribe drugs, and move on.

And when those drugs cause damage?

They prescribe more drugs to fix the damage caused by the first drug.

It's a never-ending cycle.

And I was right in the middle of it.

It's a debate I'd love to have with anyone, whether they agree or disagree.

Do doctors genuinely believe in the medications they prescribe?

Or are they just following orders from a system that prioritises profit over health?

Do pharmaceutical companies really want to cure people?

Or do they design drugs to create lifelong customers?

I don't have the perfect answers.

But I do know one thing:

The system is broken.

But for now I will continue with my story.

Because the worst was still ahead of me.

The pain.

The withdrawals.

The absolute destruction of my skin and nervous system.

Everything was about to get worse.

Much, much worse.

"The cycle begins, blisters and cracks taking over my hands. Long before I knew anything about TSW"

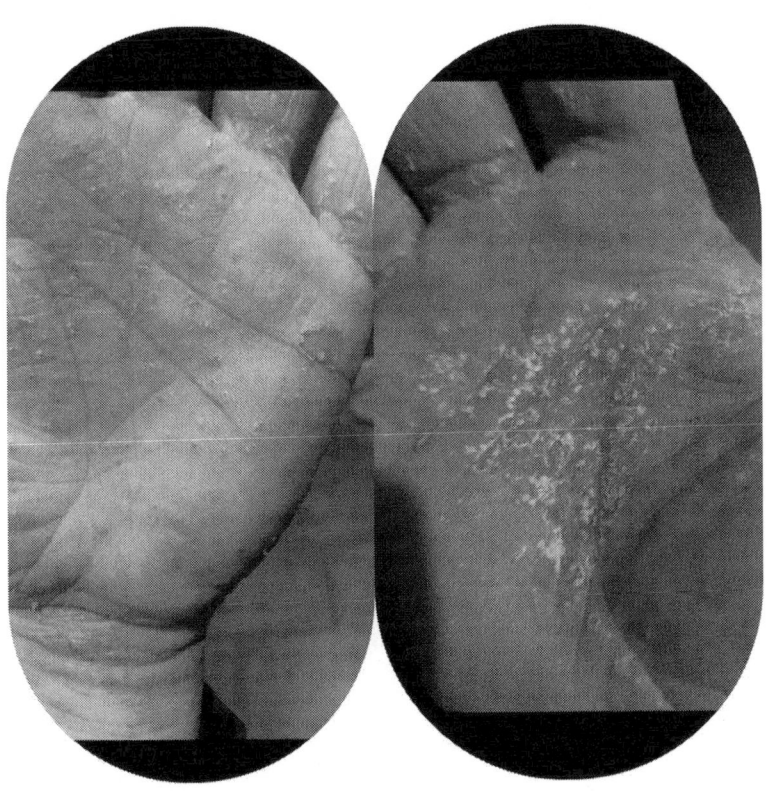

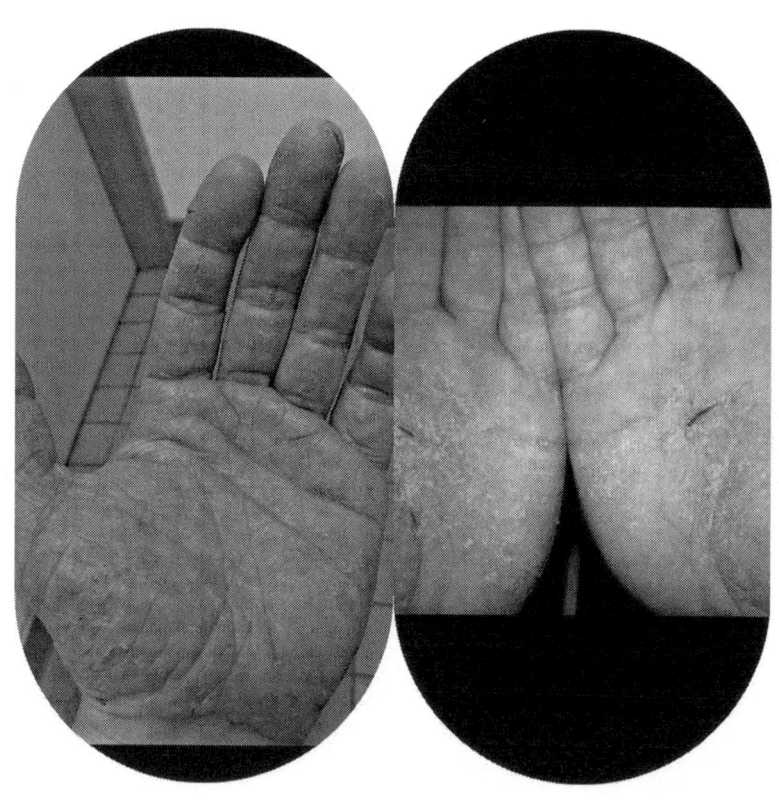

This is 2 photo's put together from the same time, during steroid use. The symmetry on both hands, the redness, the swelling and the itch was insane at this point.

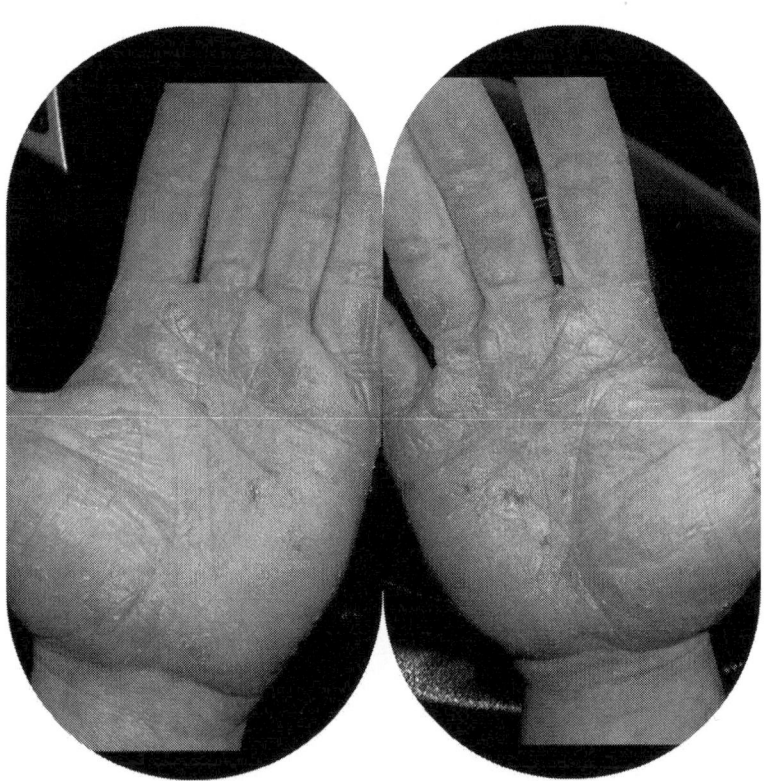

Chapter 3. Dermatologist Appointments

Chapter 3:01. The Slippery Slope

The cycle continued, turning into a downward spiral.
By eight months in, my hands were unrecognisable. What
had started as a few scattered blisters had multiplied into
full-blown clusters, spreading across my entire palms and
fingers like an unstoppable force. The blister cycle
repeating it's self, but a little worse each time it did.
The pain was relentless.
The hands was just the start, soon my feet followed.
At first, I noticed a dull, tingling itch on the arches of my
feet, an odd discomfort between my toes. Then came the
blisters, exactly like the ones on my hands, perfectly
mirroring them as if my body was fighting against itself.
My heels thickened, at first, I thought this was my skin
trying to protect itself. But instead of becoming stronger,
the skin became dry, brittle, and unforgiving. Instead of
cushioning my steps, it cracked apart, forming deep, open
fissures.
This wasn't just an irritation anymore. This wasn't just a
bad rash. This was something far worse, something that
was creeping into every part of my life, destroying it piece
by piece.
This wasn't just about my skin anymore.
This thing, whatever it was, was taking over my life.

At first, it was just blisters and cracks, just a bit of pain, just something annoying. But by now, it was turning into something much bigger. Something that affected everything, my job, my home life, my relationships, my ability to just be a normal person.

I wasn't just losing my skin. I was losing control.

3:02. The Daily Struggles - When Everything Becomes a Challenge

It robbed me of the smallest, most basic things. The kind of things you never think about until they're gone.
I couldn't hold my kids' hands. Not properly, not without wincing.
Something so simple, so natural, had become a source of pain. I wanted to squeeze their hands in mine, hold onto them tightly like I always had. But I couldn't.
If I gripped too hard, the skin would split open. If they moved suddenly, I'd feel a sharp tear across my palms.
I had to tell them, "Be gentle with Daddy's hands."
But how do you explain that to a child? How do you tell your own kids that touching you hurts?
Water had become my enemy.
Hot burned, cold tightened, and even soap, something so simple, felt unbearable. Washing my hands stung every time, and showers became something I had to prepare myself for, knowing they would only bring more discomfort."

I was embarrassed. Ashamed.

I didn't want to answer questions. Didn't want to deal with the pity in their eyes when they saw my hands.

Even if people didn't say anything, I could feel them noticing. Their eyes would flicker down to my fingers, to the cracked, peeling skin. Some would try to act normal, some would change the subject quickly, and others would outright ask, "What happened to your hands?"

I got tired of answering. I got tired of pretending I was fine. So I stopped seeing people.

3:03. The Mental Toll - The Pain You Don't See

The physical symptoms were bad enough. But what it did to my mind? That was worse.

I felt like a burden. I could see it, the extra weight my wife was carrying, picking up the slack, doing things I should have been able to do. I hated it. I hated myself for it.

I was missing more and more work. I tried to fight through it. Tried to push on. But some mornings, it was impossible. The pain was too much. The blisters too raw. But the problem with work? The bills don't care if you're in pain.

I was losing control of my life. It felt like I was being dragged under, like I was falling behind while the rest of the world kept moving forward. I had always been the strong one, the provider, the man who took care of things. But now? I felt weak. Helpless.

And then came the questions. What if this never stops? What if I'm like this forever? What if this is my life now? I needed answers. I needed someone to fix me. I went back to the GP. I was desperate. But I had no idea that the real nightmare was only just beginning.

3:04. The Last GP Appointment - A Question That Will Never Be Answered

I sat in the chair, my hands outstretched in front of me. Ruined.

The skin was raw, cracked, barely holding together. The deep fissures in my fingers made every movement feel like tearing open an old wound. My palms, once smooth and strong, were now covered in clusters of burning blisters, the skin peeling away in angry red patches.

And then there were my feet.

I slipped off my shoes and socks, revealing the splitting skin, the deep cuts on my heels, the blistered arches that made every step feel like torture.

I didn't even need to explain the pain. It was written all over me.

I looked up at the GP, waiting for some kind of reaction, a flicker of concern, a moment of realisation.

But all I got was a frown, a brief pause, just like always.
Looking back at that moment now, I wonder, did he
ever realise what he had done?

Did he ever look at my medical history, see the months
of escalating treatments, and think: Did I cause this? Did
I push too many prescriptions, too fast, without ever
questioning why?

Or did he, like I did at the time, just assume this was
some mystery skin condition that had appeared out of
nowhere?

I think about that moment a lot. I think about how he
looked at me, like I was just another patient in his long
list of appointments.

Did he think he had done his best? Did he go home that
night and forget about me completely? Or did he ever
have a brief moment where he thought back to my case,
thought about how I had started with a tiny, harmless
spot and somehow ended up here?

Because if he did, he never showed it.

Not once did he say: "Ryan, let's take a step back and
rethink this." "Maybe the steroids are making this
worse." "Maybe we should stop everything and see what
happens."

Instead, he did what he always did. He handed me
another prescription.

But this time? It wasn't for more steroids.

This time, he finally admitted that this was beyond him.

"This isn't clearing up like I expected," he muttered,
scribbling something onto the paper.

He didn't look me in the eye. He just passed me the
referral slip like it was a golden ticket.

"You're being referred to a dermatologist," he said.

"They'll figure out what's going on."

That was it.

That was his answer after eight months of watching me deteriorate.

Not an apology. Not a moment of reflection. Not even a second of acknowledgment that every single prescription he had handed me had only made me worse. Just a referral. Just a transfer of responsibility. As if everything that had happened wasn't his doing? As if it had all just been bad luck.

I took the paper, walked out of that office, and never went back. I never saw that doctor again.

And at the time? I still trusted the system.

I still believed that this was the right step. That the GP had done his best, and now, the real experts would take over.

 The dermatologists, the people who specialised in skin, who had spent years studying it, would finally see what was wrong and fix me.

I actually thought, "This is it. I'm finally going to get better."

I couldn't have been more wrong.

Because what lay ahead?

Would make everything before this. The blisters. The cracking skin. The relentless, mind-breaking itch, Feel like the calm before the storm.

3:05. The First Dermatology Appointment - New Prescriptions & Empty Promises

When the letter arrived with my first dermatology appointment at Canterbury Hospital Dermatology Department, I felt something I hadn't felt in months. Hope.

I went in thinking, finally, the experts will take over. Finally, I'll get real answers.

Instead?

It was the start of three more years of hell.

The dermatologist glanced at my hands, asked a few routine questions, and handed me a prescription. No curiosity. No deeper questions. Just another round of drugs.

Elocon (Mometasone Furoate) - A potent topical steroid, stronger than Betnovate, designed to reduce inflammation quickly. It was meant for short-term use but was never explained as such.

Prednisone (Oral Steroid Tablets) - A systemic steroid, stronger than anything I'd ever taken before. It suppresses the entire immune system and was prescribed at a high dose with a two-week tapering plan.

New Moisturisers - Another set of lotions that would do nothing but sit on the surface.

I walked out of that appointment relieved.

"This is it," I thought. "They know what they're doing. I'll be better soon."

3:06. What Is Prednisone? (And What They Never Told Me About It)

This was the most powerful steroid I had taken so far. Prednisone isn't a cream. It doesn't just sit on the skin; it works from the inside out. It's a corticosteroid, meaning it shuts down the body's natural immune response. It's used for conditions like severe inflammation, autoimmune diseases, and allergic reactions, things that need aggressive intervention.

The dermatologist never explained what Prednisone was actually doing. He only told me:

"This will stop the flare."

What he didn't tell me?

Moon Face - A common side effect where fluid retention bloats the face, making it round and swollen.

Severe Weight Gain - Prednisone slows metabolism and redistributes fat, causing rapid weight gain in the stomach and face.

Weakened Immune System - It suppresses the body's ability to fight infections, making you vulnerable to illnesses, viruses, and even fungal overgrowth.

Bone Loss (Osteoporosis) - Long-term use can weaken bones, leading to fractures.

Adrenal Suppression - The body stops producing its own cortisol, making you dependent on steroids to function.

The most dangerous part?

Once you start long-term steroid use, your adrenal glands shut down. This means you can't just stop taking Prednisone abruptly.

Doing so can cause Adrenal Crisis, a life-threatening condition where the body goes into shock, unable to produce cortisol naturally.

But I didn't know any of this.

Because no one told me.

All I knew was that I wanted to be better so I took every pill as prescribed.

3:07. Biopsy & More Confusion

Alongside my new prescriptions, the dermatologist also ordered a biopsy of the original spot on my arm, the tiny, harmless-looking mark that had started this entire nightmare.

I sat there as they numbed the area, then cut deep into my skin, almost like coring an apple, removing a cylindrical sample for testing.

It was deep enough to leave a scar.

They told me I'd have to wait a week for results.

At that point, though, my hands and feet were my biggest concern.

A week later, I got the call.

The results?

"Benign findings. No abnormalities."

That tiny, annoying spot, the one that had triggered this entire journey?

Nothing.

Just a minor irritation.

It had healed completely on its own after the biopsy.

Never to return.

But my hands and feet?

They were getting worse every day.

3:08. The Prednisone Effect - A Temporary High

I started Prednisone that same day.

By day three, I noticed a difference.

By day five, my skin looked better than it had in months.

The blisters shrank.

The redness faded.

The splits on my hands and feet finally started to close.

It was like magic.

I looked at my reflection in the mirror and thought,
"Wow, this is actually working."

For two weeks, I felt almost normal again.

For two weeks, I thought I had beaten this.

For two weeks, I allowed myself to believe that this was
the end of my suffering.

Then, the tapering started.

The dermatologist had given me a strict two-week
tapering plan, reducing my dose little by little.

By the time I got to the final few pills, I noticed
something.

The symptoms started creeping back.

The blisters returned.

The cracks deepened.

The itch, oh God, the itch, was back with a vengeance.

And by the time the two weeks were over?

I was right back where I started.

Within days, I was flaring worse than before.

I remember sitting on the edge of my bed, staring at my hands, and feeling defeated.

"What the hell just happened?"

How could I have been so much better only a few days ago?

And now be worse than ever?

3:09. The Reality of Steroid Use - What No One Warns You About

Steroids don't heal; they hide. They push symptoms down, only to let them explode when you stop. Prednisone was no different. The flares returned stronger, my body more desperate.   Doctors call it 'rebound inflammation.' I call it hell.

Because once you've felt the relief that steroids bring, you're willing to chase that relief again.

So when the flare returned, what did I do?

I went back to the dermatologist.

At this point, I still believed the doctors knew best.

I still believed they had the answers.

I still believed that each new prescription would be the one to finally cure me.

I was about to learn just how wrong I was.

3:10. The Second Dermatology Appointment - A Desperate Plan

I sat there in the cold, sterile room, my hands resting in my lap, cracked, raw, and wrapped in bandages that did nothing to stop the pain. My feet throbbed inside my shoes, the pressure of simply existing making every nerve feel like it was on fire.

The dermatologist sat across from me, flicking through my file with the detachment of someone checking a grocery list. His face was unreadable, his movements robotic. He barely glanced at me before delivering his solution, as if reading from a script.

"If you start flaring, just use the Elocon."

"We'll start you on another course of Prednisone."

"We'll see you in a month."

That was it.

No discussion. No deeper investigation. No recognition that I was sitting there in front of him, falling apart.

I wanted to scream. I wanted to grab the prescription pad out of his hands and shove it back at him. Can't you see what's happening to me?

But I didn't.

Because by this point, I knew it wouldn't matter.

I took the prescriptions without a word. Another month of blind hope. Another cycle of pretending this might work.

And as I walked out of that office, gripping those slips

of paper like they held the key to my survival, I told myself, just one more round.

One more month. One more treatment.

But deep down? I knew I was lying to myself.

Within days, everything fell apart.

3:11. The Flaring Gets Worse - A Breaking Point

I followed their instructions to the letter.

Elocon, twice a day, thin layers coating my hands and feet.

Prednisone, swallowed like a lifeline, praying it would pull me back from the edge.

Moisturisers, slathered on religiously, desperate to stop my skin from cracking open.

But it didn't help.

Nothing helped.

Same again within a week, I was right back where I started.

The blisters returned, larger, angrier, and more painful.

The splits deepened, crimson lines splitting through my palms and heels, bleeding with every step.

The burning sensation grew unbearable, like my skin was dissolving in acid.

And this time?

Even the Prednisone wasn't enough.

Before, at least, it had bought me a couple of weeks of

relief. Now, the flares came roaring back before I even finished the course. It was as if my body had stopped responding altogether, like the drugs had finally lost their grip.

Then, something new. Something no one had warned me about.

One morning, I stood in front of the bathroom mirror, staring at my reflection, and I saw it.

My face had changed.

I leaned in, running a trembling hand over my jawline, except my jawline was gone.

My cheeks were swollen, rounded, and almost unrecognisable. My entire face looked, inflated.

I blinked, stepping back. Was this really me?

It hit me like a punch to the stomach.

"What the hell is happening to me?"

Later, I learned the name for it, Moon Face.

Fluid retention.

Fat redistribution.

A face that didn't even look like mine anymore.

I had been so focused on the pain in my hands and feet, so consumed by the daily agony, that I hadn't even noticed what the steroids were doing to the rest of me.

It didn't matter that my skin was still falling apart. It didn't matter that my body felt like it was rotting from the inside.

All I could see was the stranger in the mirror.

Because this wasn't just about my skin anymore.

I was losing myself.

3:12. A New Drug - The Moment I Let Go of Control

By the time I sat in that dermatologist's office again, I was barely holding on.

The Prednisone had failed me.

The Elocon had failed me.

My own body had failed me.

The dermatologist barely glanced at me before flipping through my file, months of failed treatments reduced to ink on paper. No hesitation, no second thoughts. 'We'll start you on Azathioprine,' he said.

"Just another drug. Just another gamble, I thought"

I frowned. Azathioprine?

"What's that?"

"An immunosuppressant. It will help regulate your immune system and keep the flares under control long-term."

"Is it safe?"

"Yes, it's used for autoimmune diseases all the time. It will help."

That was all he said.

No warnings. No discussion of side effects. No hesitation.

Just another prescription. Another blind leap.

And I took it.

I didn't hesitate. I didn't ask for details.

Because at that moment? I didn't care.

I was done fighting. Done questioning. Done hoping.

I just wanted it to end.

So I agreed.

And that was the moment I gave up control of my own body.

3:13. What Is Azathioprine? (And What They Never Told Me About It)

Azathioprine is not just another medication. It's a powerful immunosuppressant, originally developed for organ transplant patients.

When someone receives a new organ, their immune system attacks it, seeing it as a foreign object. Azathioprine stops this attack by shutting down the immune system.

For people with autoimmune conditions, dermatologists prescribe it to suppress inflammation by forcing the immune system into submission. It was supposed to help me. It was supposed to fix everything.

But what they didn't tell me? It was one of the most dangerous drugs I would ever take.

Side Effects & Risks of Azathioprine.
This wasn't just some mild drug. This was a serious medication with serious risks.

Severely Weakened Immune System.

61

Even a simple cold could turn into something dangerous. A minor infection could become life-threatening.

Nausea & Vomiting.

Many patients struggle to keep food down.

Constant stomach issues, waves of sickness.

Liver Toxicity.

Requires regular blood tests, because it can cause liver damage.

If levels spike too high? Liver failure.

Increased Cancer Risk

Higher rates of lymphoma and skin cancer in long-term users.
What they didn't tell me
"We need to monitor your blood every few weeks."
"We need to check your liver function regularly."
"There's a risk of long-term immune suppression."
Did they tell me any of this before I agreed? No.
They just handed me the prescription and sent me on my way.
And at that moment? I didn't care. Because all I knew was that the dermatologist said it would help. And I was desperate.
So I took it.
At first? It seemed like it was working. For the first time

in a long time? I thought maybe, just maybe, this was the answer. I thought maybe this was the light at the end of the tunnel.

But I had no idea. That tunnel? It was about to collapse..

The last photo I can find with 2 of my kids before the hell. This was a break we managed to get why the azathioprine worked for a bit.
My face is still slightly swollen from the prednisone and more red than it had been previously

3:14. The Cycle Returns - A Nightmare Without an End

A couple of months passed. I followed every instruction. I took the Azathioprine every as prescribed. I had routine blood tests. I was doing everything they told me to do. And at first, it seemed like things were under control. The flares were milder.

The blisters didn't appear as aggressively.

The deep cracks weren't as constant.
I clung to that progress like a lifeline.
But then it happened. The same cycle, the one I had lived through over and over, came crashing back.
Slight improvement, then a massive flare-up.

The blisters returned, bigger, deeper, and more painful.

The cracks in my skin felt like they were splitting open even wider.

My skin was becoming thinner, weaker.
And this time? This time, it was worse than ever.
Something felt different this time. It wasn't just my skin anymore.
For the first time in my life, I felt constantly ill.
I felt drained all the time, like I was carrying around a lead weight on my back.
I started catching random sickness bugs, minor colds that hit me like the flu.

My body felt weaker, like I had no strength, no reserves left.

I had no idea why I was feeling like this.

But the truth? My immune system was being destroyed. The very medication that was supposed to help me heal was actually shutting down my body's defenses.

And I had gone from steroid addiction to full immune suppression. My skin was STILL getting worse.

3:15. The Breaking Point - A Realisation Too Late

I sat alone in my own thought's, trying to process everything.

I had followed their instructions. I had taken the medications exactly as prescribed. I had done everything they told me to do.

And yet, I was worse than ever.

For months, I had clung to the belief that they knew what they were doing. That they had my best interests at heart. That these drugs were the answer.

But now? Now I was starting to question everything.

Was this really the best they could do? Or had I just spent the last two years being led down a path that was never going to heal me?

Something had to change. And deep down, I knew that no doctor was going to save me. If I wanted to get better? I had to figure this out myself.

By this point, I didn't know what to do anymore. Every day felt like I was trapped in a never-ending battle.

There was no progress.

There was no relief.

There was no light at the end of the tunnel.

I couldn't see a way forward.
I had no energy left to fight.
And worst of all?
I felt like I was failing my family.

3.16. The Toll On My Home Life

The atmosphere at home had changed.
I wasn't the husband and father I had been before.
The fun, joking, outgoing Ryan? He was gone.

The hardworking provider, always pushing forward? He was gone too.

And in his place?

A man who could barely get through the day.

A man who spent more time in bed than out of it.

A man who was watching his own life slip through his fingers.

66

Ryan Thomson
The Eczema Deception

I couldn't play with my kids' properly, because my skin
would split open at the slightest touch of anything.
I couldn't even do simple tasks around the house,
because touching anything, even water, felt like fire.
And I could see it in their eyes.
They didn't fully understand what was happening to me.
But they knew I wasn't the same.
I was withdrawing, isolating myself more and more.
And the worst part?
People could see the damage.
But they could never feel what I was going through.
They couldn't feel:
The constant, unbearable itch.

The raw, burning sensation, like my skin had been torn
off.

The deep, open splits, so painful that even the air hitting
them made me wince.
This was not just skin irritation.
This was not just discomfort.
This was a new level of misery, one I wouldn't have
wished on my worst enemy.
Every movement of my hands was agony.

Every step I took was torture.

Every minute of every day was consumed by pain,
irritation, exhaustion, and frustration.
I had lost control of my own body.

And worse?

I had lost control of my own life.

How had I ended up here?

How had I gone from a single spot?

To this?

I had trusted the doctors.

I had trusted the medication.

I had done everything they told me to do.

And now?

I was worse than ever.

And I was about to hit rock bottom.

3:17 A New Hope - Or Another Risk?

We had stopped the azathioprine as this was only
making me feel sick and no longer helping the skin.

The dermatologist had suggested a new drug, Toctino.

By this point, I had lost count of how many medications
I had tried.

Nothing had worked.

Nothing had lasted.

And I was desperate.

So when they told me about Toctino, I barely hesitated.

But there was a problem.

This wasn't like the other prescriptions.

This wasn't a cream I could pick up from the pharmacy
or a tablet I could start that same day.

Toctino required special funding approval, and that could

take weeks.

Even months.

And in the meantime?

I was still suffering.

I remember sitting there, nodding as the dermatologist explained the process, but all I could think was: "How long do I have to wait?"

"How much worse will I get in that time?"

"Will this finally be the thing that saves me?"

The dermatologist explained that Toctino was not a steroid.

That alone made me listen carefully.

For the first time, this wasn't another potent topical cream, another round of Prednisone, or another immune suppressant that made me sick.

This was different.

It was used for severe chronic hand eczema.

It worked by regulating skin cell production and reducing inflammation.

It had helped people who hadn't responded to steroids.

It sounded promising.

But what they didn't do?

They didn't fully explain the risks.

3:18. What Is Toctino? (What I Didn't Know at the Time)

Toctino (Alitretinoin) is a powerful retinoid. If that word sounds familiar, it's because it's closely related to Accutane, the infamous drug used to treat severe acne. It doesn't just reduce inflammation; it completely alters the way skin cells develop and shed.

That's why it requires strict monitoring. That's why it's not given out easily. And that's why it comes with a list of serious side effects.

Side Effects of Toctino - The Risks I Didn't Consider

At the time, I was so focused on relief that I didn't question what I was getting into. But Toctino isn't just another pill, it's a high-risk medication with serious consequences.

Some of the most severe risks include:

Liver Damage - Patients on Toctino require frequent liver function tests because the drug can cause toxicity.

Severe Headaches & Migraines - Many people on Toctino suffer from relentless, intense headaches.

Mood Changes & Depression - Retinoids like Toctino have been linked to increased depression and suicidal thoughts.

Dry, Peeling Skin - The drug can dry out the skin so much that it becomes cracked, painful, and worse than before.

Birth Defects - Toctino is extremely dangerous for pregnant women, requiring strict birth control measures for anyone taking it.

But back then? I didn't care. I didn't ask questions. I

didn't hesitate. I just wanted relief.

3:19. The Waiting Game

Approval took weeks, weeks of flaring, weeks of waiting, weeks of pain that no one else had to endure. While the system moved at its own pace, my body continued to fall apart.

Would this be the answer? Or was I just signing up for another disaster?
I had no way of knowing. All I could do was wait, and hope.

Toctino wasn't like the other prescriptions I had been given before. This wasn't a quick fix or a simple pick-up from the pharmacy. This was expensive, and because of that, the NHS wasn't going to hand it out without approval.
So I had to wait. And wait. And while I was waiting? I was still worsening by the day.
The funding application took weeks.
Weeks of waking up to burning, splitting skin. Weeks of struggling to work, to walk, to do basic things around the house. Weeks of trying to hold onto some form of hope, even as my condition kept deteriorating.
I found myself wondering:

"Why does it have to be like this?" "Why do we have to wait to be approved for relief?" "Why is it that the worse we get, the longer they make us suffer before we can try something new?"

I knew there were people far worse off than me, people waiting months or even years for essential treatments.

But that didn't make it any easier.

Because when you're in pain every second of the day, time moves differently.

Every day of suffering feels like a week. Every week feels like a month.

And while the bureaucracy played out, I realised something else:

I couldn't carry on like this, not just with my treatment, but with my job.

3:20. Changing Jobs - A Tough but Necessary Decision

At this point, I knew one thing for certain:

I couldn't continue doing price work.

I had spent years working in construction, moving from site to site, pushing myself to work fast and work hard.

But every single day on-site had become a battle against my own body.

The gloves made my hands sweat, triggering fresh itching and blistering. The dust and dirt aggravated my already raw and inflamed skin. The physical labour took its toll,

leaving me exhausted beyond belief.
I was trying to work through the pain, but it was beating me down. And I had to admit; I couldn't keep up anymore.

3:21. A New Opportunity - The Right Job at the Right Time

That's when I started talking to my best mate from school, Neil Langmaid.
Neil had been working as the building manager for UPP, a company responsible for managing over 2,000 student accommodations, including plant rooms, kitchens, and maintenance facilities.
For years, UPP had been outsourcing their electrical work. But now? They wanted to bring in their own full-time electrician.
And at that exact time? I was already working on a UPP student accommodation project.
It felt like it was meant to be.
The job paid less than what I had been making as a self-employed electrician. But when I factored in all the days I was losing due to my condition? The difference wasn't that much.
More importantly? They paid me for hospital appointments. That alone made all the difference.
So I went for the interview, and I got the job.
It was a tough choice, but deep down, I knew:
I needed stability more than I needed higher pay. I needed time to focus on my health. And most of all, I

needed to stop fighting against my own body every single day.

For the first time in a long time, I felt like I was making a decision that would actually help me.

Now, all I could do was wait for the funding to come through, and hope that Toctino would be the answer I had been searching for.

3:22. The Reality Of Toctiono - More Monitoring, More Uncertainty

Once my funding was finally approved, I was immediately started on Toctino.

But this wasn't like the other medications I had been on.

Strict monitoring was mandatory. For the first six weeks, I had to have weekly blood tests and blood pressure checks. After that, The testing became less frequent, but I was still required to attend regular check-ups.

The reason? Toctino could be dangerous.

The risk of liver damage, severe headaches, mood changes, and other side effects meant that every patient on Toctino had to be watched closely.

At this point, I had already been through hell with previous treatments. And now, I was back to feeling like a lab experiment.

More hospital visits.

More waiting rooms.

More stress.

And the biggest concern of all? What if this didn't work either?

3:23. The First Three Months - Temporary Hope

For three months, Toctino gave me a glimpse of normality. The cracks weren't as deep, the blisters less aggressive. I let myself believe, maybe this was it. Maybe I had found the answer. Then, like every other treatment before it, Toctino failed. The blisters roared back, the burning relentless. The cycle wasn't over. It was just getting started.

By this point, I had lost faith in the entire system.

I had spent years trusting doctors.

Years following instructions.

Years taking every prescription they handed me.

Yet, I was worse than ever.

Every single treatment I had tried, topical steroids, oral steroids, immunosuppressant's, retinoids, had only pushed me further into suffering.

Every promise of relief was a lie.

Every new prescription only led to more pain.

Every visit to the doctor gave me hope, only for it to be ripped away.

And still, no one could explain why this was happening to me.

At home, I searched online for hours, night after night,

75

desperate to find someone, anyone, who had been through the same thing.

But everything I found just repeated the same medical advice the dermatologists had been telling me for years:

"Use your steroid creams consistently."

"Moisturise regularly."

"Consider another immunosuppressant."

None of it made sense anymore.

If I had followed everything correctly, then why was I still getting worse?

The Allergy Tests - A Dead End

I even went through patch testing three times at Canterbury Hospital.

Hundreds of substances, fragrances, preservatives, metals, chemicals, foods, were tested on my skin.

Not a single allergy came up.

No contact dermatitis.

No food intolerances.

No hidden allergies.

There was never anything actually wrong with me.

How did this happen?

One small spot on my arm.

One five-minute visit to the GP.

One mild steroid cream.

And now?

Four years later, I was barely surviving.

The same hands that had built my career, that had held my children, that had been strong enough to work long hours, were now too raw to even function.

Ryan Thomson
The Eczema Deception

I had gone from a healthy, active father to someone who could barely walk without pain, work without suffering, or sleep without scratching himself raw.

I was a shadow of myself.
Nothing excited me anymore.
Nothing made me feel like "me."
Because every single day was just pain, discomfort, and stress.
I was completely lost.

The hands, continued to get worse and worse, and I didn't know what to do for the best

And sorry if these photos are not nice to look at, but this was my reality, it was worse to go through than to look at.

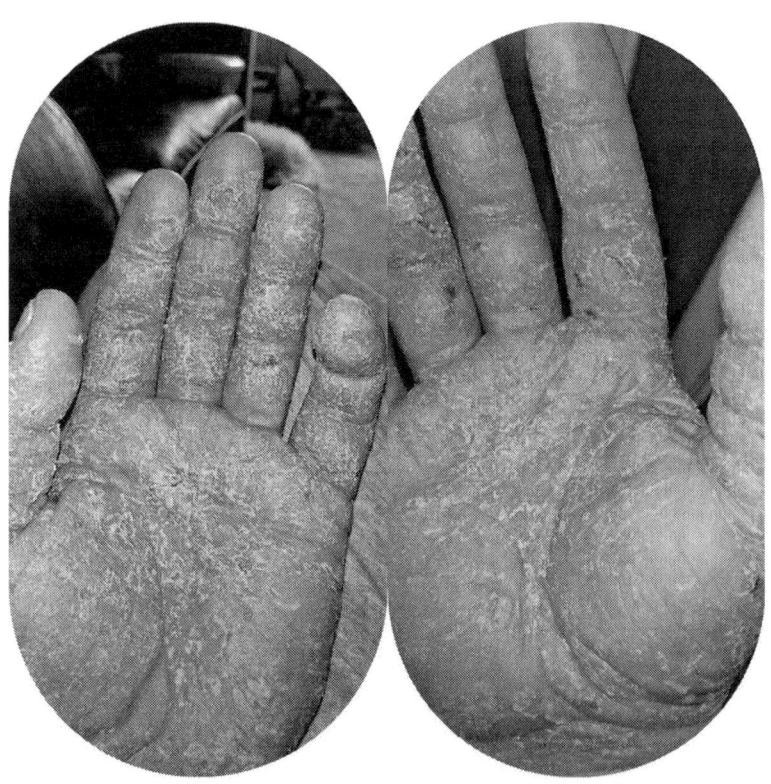

And this was whilst still on medication to make me
BETTTER!!

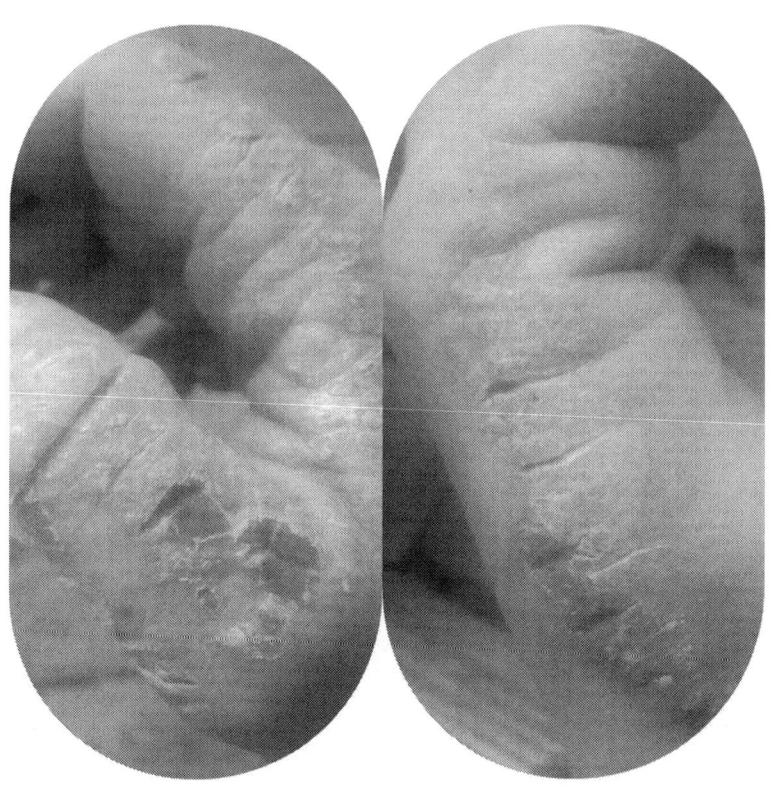

Chapter 4. When My Eyes Was Opened

4:01. Discovering The Truth

By this point, I was at my absolute breaking point.
There was no relief.
No comfort.
No escape.
Every single waking moment was ruled by one thing, my skin. The cycle was never-ending:
Splitting open.
Healing slightly.
Then splitting again.
Over and over. It felt like my body was trapped in an endless loop of self-destruction.
No other part of my body was affected. It was just my hands and feet. That only made things more confusing.
Why just my hands and feet?
Why wasn't this happening anywhere else?
What the hell was going on with me?
It made no sense. The doctors had no answers. And I was starting to realise, neither did I.

4:02. Barely Holding on at Work

I wasn't just struggling; I was barely surviving. I was getting slower, the work harder, and for someone who took pride in their skill, it was demoralising.

Every movement of my hands was like dragging a razor blade across an open wound. Yet, I had to keep going. Because what other option did I have?

And it wasn't just my hands. My feet were under attack, too.

The deep cracks in my feet made walking a challenge. Every step sent pain shooting up my legs, sharp, unbearable, suffocating. But stopping wasn't an option. I had to get to work.

I had to support my family.

I had to keep going, no matter how much it hurt.

At first, I tried to hide it. I gritted my teeth and pushed through. I forced myself to move faster, even though I could feel my skin splitting. I ignored the blood, the stinging, and the agony, because I had no choice.

But no matter what I did, I was falling behind. And deep down, I knew it.

Ryan, the one my family and friends knew?

He was gone.

It was all getting way too much for me.

I wasn't just losing my skin. I was losing myself.

How much longer can I keep this up?

81

I didn't have the answers. But one thing was for certain, I couldn't live like this much longer.

4:03. Isolation & Anger

I faded into the background. Friends? I had no energy for them. Small talk? Impossible. Even at home, I wasn't present. My family laughed, played, carried on, but I was just there. Watching, aching, and sinking.

No jokes, no excitement, no joy. Just surviving, not living.

It was relentless. The discomfort never stopped. There was no break, no moment of relief. I couldn't switch off from it, not for a second.

I would wake up in pain.

I would go to work in pain.

I would eat dinner in pain.

I would lie in bed at night, tired, desperate for sleep, but the itch would never let me rest.

It consumed every single part of my day. I tried to distract myself, but it was impossible to. I couldn't enjoy watching TV, I couldn't even sit down for five minutes without being painfully aware of my skin.

At night, when the world was silent and I was alone with my thoughts, that's when it was the worst. I would lay in the dark, staring at the ceiling, my entire body buzzing with discomfort. Scratching was pointless, but not scratching was unbearable. It was a never-ending battle that I always lost.

I had forgotten what it felt like to be comfortable.

4:04. The Well-Meaning but Clueless Advice

Then there were the people, the ones with all the answers, despite never having been through this.
'Try coconut oil!'
'Just moisturise more!'
'My cousin used Aveeno, it worked wonders!'
I wanted to scream at them "do you not think I have tried everything I possibly can"
They meant well, but they had no idea.
They didn't know what it was like to wake up every morning feeling like your skin was on fire.
They didn't know what it was like to have your hands so cracked and raw that you couldn't even tie your own shoelaces.
They didn't know what it was like to dread taking a shower because water felt like acid on your skin.
I knew they meant well. I really did. But they weren't helping. They didn't understand that this wasn't just dry skin. This wasn't just eczema. This was my entire life falling apart in front of me, I had never felt so alone in my entire life. I had never felt so hopeless.
And at this point, I thought I had reached the peak of my suffering. I thought this was as bad as it was going to get. But I was wrong.
The real suffering hadn't even begun yet.

4:05. The Endless Cycle - Another Drug, Another Failure

By this point, I had lost all faith in the medical system. Everything they had told me, every prescription they had given me, every so-called "treatment" had led me right back to where I started, or worse.

I was exhausted.

Mentally.

Physically.

Emotionally.

Every ounce of hope I had was gone.

After Toctino failed, they put me on yet another drug, Ciclosporin.

At this stage, I had stopped researching these medications before I took them. What was the point? Every single one had followed the same pattern.

A short-lived improvement.

A return to the same symptoms.

A gradual decline into an even worse state than before.

And Ciclosporin was no different.

4:06. Ciclosporin - Another Immunosuppressant

Ciclosporin is a powerful immunosuppressant, originally developed for organ transplant patients.

Its primary function? To prevent the body from rejecting transplanted organs by shutting down the immune system.

But in dermatology, it's often prescribed for severe eczema and psoriasis, with the idea that suppressing the immune response will stop the inflammation.

On the surface, it sounded promising.

"If my skin issues are immune-related, wouldn't suppressing the immune system solve the problem?"

"But won't this just be the same as the azathioprine?"

But as I had learned the hard way, nothing was ever that simple.

The Risks & Side Effects of Ciclosporin,

Ciclosporin isn't a mild medication. It's a serious, high-risk drug that requires constant monitoring.

Kidney damage - Long-term use is highly toxic to the kidneys, requiring frequent blood tests.

High blood pressure - It puts strain on the heart, increasing cardiovascular risks.

Increased risk of infections - With a weakened immune system, even a simple cold could become dangerous.

Gum overgrowth - A bizarre but common side effect, causing swollen, enlarged gums.

Cancer risk - Long-term use has been linked to lymphoma and skin cancers.

But at this stage? I didn't even care anymore.

I just wanted relief.

And at first, I got it.

The False Hope of Ciclosporin.

The first few weeks on Ciclosporin were a breath of fresh air.

My skin calmed down.

The blisters faded slightly.

The cracks on my hands and feet weren't as deep.

The constant burning and itching dulled a little.

For the first time in in a long time, I felt like I could function again.

But I had been here before.

I knew better than to get too excited.

And sure enough, the cycle repeated itself.

After about two months, the symptoms came creeping back.

Slowly at first.

Then all at once.

And just like that?

I was back to square one.

Except this time, my body had endured yet another toxic medication with no benefit.

4:07. Running Out of Options

By this point, I had seen four or five different dermatologists over the years at Canterbury Hospital. Each one had their own approach, but the treatment plans were always the same:

Topical steroids - Every strength, every type.

Oral steroids – Prednisone, short courses, long tapers.

Immunosuppressants - Azathioprine, Ciclosporin.

Retinoids - Toctino.

Moisturisers - Dozens of different brands.

Nothing worked.

Absolutely nothing.

I had followed every single instruction the doctors gave me.

I had trusted every medication they prescribed.

I had done everything I was told to do.

And yet, I was still getting worse.

How was that possible?

"If they're the experts, why can't they fix this?"

"Why does every treatment make me worse in the long run?"

I was out of options.

And for the first time,

I started to wonder if the doctors had been wrong all along.

4:08. The Realisation That Changed Everything

For years, I had walked into appointments expecting answers.

Expecting solutions.

Expecting that, at some point, someone would figure out what was happening to me.

But now?

I could see it in their eyes, the hesitation, the uncertainty, the way they glanced at my chart and back at me as if hoping something would magically make sense.

They weren't in control anymore.

They were guessing.

They had followed their protocols to the letter.

They had prescribed every treatment in their arsenal, checked every box on their checklist.

But none of it had worked.

And the worst part?

They had no idea why.

I sat there, skin raw, hands and feet wrecked beyond recognition, and for the first time,

I realised, they weren't going to fix this. Because they didn't know how!!

4:09. How Did It Get This Far?

I replayed everything in my head.

How did a healthy 32-year-old man, who walked into a GP's office with one tiny spot on his arm, end up here, barely functioning at 36 years old?

How did a simple prescription for a mild steroid cream turn into years of suffering, drug after drug, treatment after treatment, all leading to this?

It made no sense.

I had gone through patch testing three times, hundreds of allergens tested against my skin. Nothing.

I had multiple blood tests, checking for every possible

condition under the sun. Everything normal.

I had followed every single piece of medical advice given to me, exactly as instructed.

And yet, I was still getting worse.

Trapped in a body that was breaking down in front of my own eyes.

Then, the anger started creeping in.

I hated my life.

I hated what I had become.

I hated that no one could explain this to me.

I hated that I had trusted these so-called experts, only to be left worse off than when I started.

I had reached my breaking point.

This wasn't just about my skin anymore.

I wasn't just losing my health.

I was losing my will to keep going.

4:10. Desperation & The Search for Answers

I had been desperately searching for answers.

Late nights turned into early mornings, my phone screen burning into my eyes as I scrolled endlessly through:

Medical websites.

Forums.

Dermatology pages.

Anywhere that might have an answer.

I wasn't just looking anymore. I was begging for a solution.

Every search led me to the same recommendations: Eczema treatments, moisturise more, use fragrance-free products, and avoid triggers.

Psoriasis treatments, biologics, vitamin D creams, phototherapy.

Chronic skin condition solutions, elimination diets, allergy testing, stress reduction.

I followed everything to the letter.

I tried every cream.

I tried every moisturiser.

I tried every so-called natural remedy.

I read articles from top dermatologists, scoured medical journals, and trusted every single word written by these so-called experts.

And that was my biggest mistake.

4:11. The Wrong Diagnosis, The Wrong Battle

I had spent years trying to fix something I didn't even have.

What if this wasn't eczema at all?

What if my body wasn't just 'flaring' because of triggers?

What if my immune system wasn't just 'overreacting' to allergens?

What if this wasn't a chronic, lifelong skin condition like they had told me?

What if everything I had been told was a lie?
For four years, I had walked down a road that led me
nowhere.

Chasing treatments that never worked.
Suppressing symptoms instead of finding the cause.
Layering medication over medication in a desperate
attempt to make it stop.
But what if I had been led down the wrong path from the
very beginning?
 I felt like I had been manipulated. Lied to.
Made to believe that my body was the problem.
But what if the real problem was the medication itself?
It was time to stop blindly believing everything I read.
It was time to start questioning everything.

4:12. The Video That Changed Everything

 One night, during another endless search for answers, I
stumbled across a video.
It wasn't like all the other "expert" advice videos I had
seen before.
It was different.
I clicked play, not knowing that this one moment would
change the entire course of my life.
 The video was by an American dermatologist named Dr.
Marvin Rapaport, and in the title were two phrases I had
never heard before:
Red Skin Syndrome (RSS)

Topical Steroid Withdrawal (TSW)

I paused.

I had spent years searching for answers, scrolling through medical forums, reading dermatology journals, trying every treatment thrown at me.

Yet I had never come across these terms before.

"My skin is red, and I have been using steroids for years, but withdrawal? How can you withdraw from ointments?"

I had no idea that this video would be the single most important thing I had ever watched.

For the first time in four years, everything was about to make sense.

Finally, A Doctor Who Understood

I would recommend anyone suffering from a chronic skin condition to watch this video.

I would urge any medical practitioner to watch it too.

Because Dr. Marvin Rapaport wasn't just talking about medical theory, he was describing my exact experience, word for word.

Every single thing he said rang true.

Every symptom, every cycle, every struggle, it was all there.

For the first time in years, I finally had an answer.

He had been fighting to raise awareness about Red Skin Syndrome (RSS) and Topical Steroid Withdrawal (TSW) for decades.

Thousands of people had gone through the exact same thing, and thousands had been cured by doing one thing: Stopping the use of topical steroids.

I sat there, glued to the screen, hanging onto every word.

Then, he said something that sent chills down my spine:

Ryan Thomson
The Eczema Deception

"The majority of people going through this are long-term eczema sufferers, but historically, eczema burns itself out by ages 5, 6, or 7 at the latest. If a person still has eczema at 25, 40, or 70, this is not eczema."

I sat there, stunned.

I had never had eczema in my life.

Not as a baby.

Not as a child.

Not as a teenager.

I was 32 years old when this all started,

How was it possible that I suddenly developed severe, uncontrollable eczema at 32?

The answer was simple:

It wasn't eczema.

It was a steroid-induced condition.

The truth about Steroids - A Wonder Drug or a Trap?

Dr. Rapaport explained that steroids can be a "wonder drug" when used correctly, short-term, for acute conditions.

But when overprescribed and used chronically, they cause extreme adverse effects.

He described the exact cycle that had ruined my life:

You get a small rash or a single spot.

You go to the pharmacy, and they give you hydrocortisone.

It gets a bit better, but not perfect, so you go to the GP.

The GP prescribes a stronger steroid.

The rash clears up, but 5 days later, it's back again.

You apply more steroid, it clears up again, but this time, it returns in just 3 days.

The cycle continues.

And before you even realise it, you are completely

addicted.

You are now a victim of the system.

You are addicted to steroids.

I sat there, frozen.

This was exactly what had happened to me.

The Dermatologists Were Looking in the Wrong Place
For years, my dermatologists had been searching for a reason behind my worsening condition.

They had suggested:

"Maybe it's leaky gut?"

"Maybe it's an unknown allergy?"

"Maybe you have an underlying autoimmune disorder?"

They were looking for everything except the real cause.

  Dr. Rapaport had the answer.

The steroids had caused this.

The very medication that was supposed to be helping was the reason I was getting worse.

The Hardest Truth - This Was Going to Take Years
As I continued watching, I heard something that terrified me.

"The cure time for Topical Steroid Withdrawal (TSW) is between 3 to 5 years."

3 to 5 years?!

I couldn't believe what I was hearing.

I had already suffered for 4 years,

Now I had to suffer for another 3 to 5 years before I would be healed?

The thought was overwhelming.

I wanted to believe it wasn't true, but every part of me knew it was.

4:13. My Research into Red Skin Syndrome & Topical Steroid Withdrawal (TSW)

After watching that video, I couldn't stop researching.
I read everything I could find about:
Red Skin Syndrome (RSS)
Topical Steroid Withdrawal (TSW)
How people recovered
The more I read, the more everything made sense.
Most people going through Topical Steroid Withdrawal
(TSW) said that the first 3 to 6 months were the worst.
After that, things slowly started to improve.
But that didn't change the questions racing through my
mind:
How bad was this going to get?
How would I work?
How would I support my family?
I felt trapped.

4:14. No One Believed Me

When something this serious is happening in your life, it
overtakes everything.
And I'm an open book, so I talked to everyone about it.
But the hardest part?

No one believed me.

My friends thought I was overthinking it.

My family thought I should just keep following the dermatologist's advice.

My GP and dermatologists dismissed it completely.

I was adamant that this was the truth.

But I was alone in this fight.

I realised something that night.

Doctors don't like to be questioned.

Dermatologists don't like to admit they're wrong.

And the system doesn't like people who go against the status quo.

For four years, I had been following blindly.

For four years, I had been trusting a system that was harming me.

And now?

Now, I knew the truth.

This wasn't eczema.

This wasn't some mystery condition.

This wasn't bad luck.

This was full-blown steroid addiction.

And the only way out was to quit steroids completely.

Now that I had the answer, a new question took over my mind:

How the hell do I survive Topical Steroid Withdrawal (TSW)?

How do I get through the worst part, the part where everything falls apart?

How do I prepare for what's coming?

Because if Dr. Rapaport was right, if I was truly about to enter the darkest phase of my life, I needed to be ready.

And that night, as I shut off my phone and lay in bed staring at the ceiling, I knew one thing for certain, "Nothing would ever be the same again"

4:15. Facing the Dermatologists

The next dermatology appointment felt different.
I wasn't going in looking for another prescription.
I wasn't hoping for another temporary fix.
I was going in with answers, real answers.
I had watched the videos.
I had done the research.
I knew what was happening to me.
And this time, I wasn't looking for their advice.
I was telling them what I was going to do.
I walked into that room feeling a mix of determination and fear.
I sat in front of them and laid it all out.
I told them about Topical Steroid Withdrawal.
I explained Red Skin Syndrome.
I went through every symptom, connecting the dots one by one.
And then, I did something I thought would convince them for sure,
I showed them Dr. Rapaport's video.
I was expecting something, shock, interest, maybe even a conversation.
But instead,
Their faces were blank.
I could see it in their expressions.

They didn't believe me.
They thought I was crazy.
There was no curiosity.
No willingness to investigate.
No concern that maybe, just maybe, they had been
wrong all along.
And then, I realised something even more terrifying.
If I stopped steroids, they had NO IDEA how to help
me.
For years, they had thrown everything at me,

- Steroids
- Immunosuppressants
- Oral medications
- Retinoids

But without those?
They had nothing.
I wasn't just on my own,
I was on my own without any medical support.
That was the moment I truly understood.
If I was going to survive this, it was all on me.

4:16. The Fear of What Was Coming

I knew I needed to do this.
I had to stop steroids.
But I was terrified.
I had no idea how bad it was going to get.
I had no idea how I would be able to work through the withdrawals.
My job gave me 20 days of sick pay per year,
and I had already used a lot of them.
What would happen when I ran out?
What if I couldn't function?
What if I physically couldn't get out of bed?
The fear of the unknown was overwhelming.
There was no guide for this.
No step-by-step treatment plan.
No one to tell me exactly what to expect.
There were only the stories of others who had gone through it.
And their stories were horrific.
I had many discussions with my wife about this.
She had been with me through all of it.
She had seen it from the beginning.
The tiny spot on my arm.
The constant trips to the GP.
The downward spiral into suffering.
She had watched me go from a healthy, strong man to a shell of myself.
She had seen my hands split open,
seen my feet bleed as I walked,
seen my skin flake away in layers.

She didn't doubt me.

She knew what was happening.

And when I told her I needed to do this
she didn't argue.

But we both knew what it meant.

It was going to be hell.

It was going to test us in ways we had never been tested
before.

We weren't just preparing for a tough few weeks.

This was years of suffering ahead.

And the scariest part?

There was no way to predict how bad it would get.

Would I be able to work?

Would I even be able to get out of bed?

Would I need full-time care?

There were no answers, only the terrifying road ahead.

 I also approached my manager at work.

I had no choice. I needed to be honest.

I sat down and told them everything.

This was going to be really hard at first.

I didn't know how bad it would get.

But I needed to do this.

I needed them to understand that my performance might
suffer.

I needed them to know that I might need time off.

I don't know if they fully agreed with me.

I don't know if they believed in what I was saying.

But at this point,

I didn't need their approval.

I didn't need their understanding.

I needed to save myself.

This was it.

I had made my decision.

There was no turning back now.

I was about to walk into the hardest battle of my life.

And the only thing I could do, was survive.

The last photo of my face before Topical Steroid Withdrawal (TSW),

2 months before I went cold turkey.

Not dry, but the red face was getting worse

Chapter 5. The Point Of No Return

5:01. The Decision Was Made

The time had come.

For years, I had trusted the system. I had put my faith in doctors, specialists, and so-called experts, believing that someone, anyone, would have the answer.

I had followed every prescription, every new treatment plan, and every dose adjustment, convinced that relief was just around the corner.

But relief never came.

Only more pain.

For months, my routine had been the same.

Get home.

Try to numb the discomfort.

Sit on my phone or laptop, scrolling endlessly.

I read through everything, looking for one person, just one, who had been through what I was going through and found a way out.

And then, I found it.

ITSAN, The International Topical Steroid Addiction Network.

Red Skin Syndrome.

Topical Steroid Withdrawal (TSW).

Three terms I had never once heard from a doctor.

Three terms that would explain everything.

5:02. The Moment Everything Clicked

I found forums filled with people just like me.
Their stories were identical to mine.

Their photos were identical to mine.
They had started with a small rash, just like I had.
They had been prescribed a mild steroid, just like I had.
They had trusted the doctors and followed every single
instruction, just like I had.
And now? They were suffering in a way that no one
could explain, just like I was.

I wasn't sick.
I wasn't broken.
I wasn't some medical mystery.
I was addicted.
Not to a drug I had willingly taken.
Not to something illegal or recreational.
I was addicted to a doctor-prescribed medication, and no
one had ever told me that this was even possible.
For the first time in five years, everything made sense.

5:03. The Truth That No One Told Me

Not a single dermatologist had mentioned this.
Not a single GP had warned me.

Not a single so-called expert had even suggested that my condition was caused by the very treatment they were giving me.
Instead, I had spent years being:
Misdiagnosed.
Given stronger and stronger steroids.
Told that my skin was the problem, not the treatment.
Handed one prescription after another like some kind of lab experiment.

And all the while, I was getting worse.
I had been conditioned to believe that this was just "severe eczema."
But now?
Now, I knew the truth.
And that truth changed everything.

5:04. What I Learned About Topical Steroid Withdrawal

For many years, I had been under the impression that steroids were completely safe. That they were the treatment for skin conditions.
But what I read shocked me to my core.
Topical Steroids: How They Work & Why They Fail
Topical steroids work by mimicking cortisol, a hormone produced by the adrenal glands. Cortisol regulates inflammation, immune response, and skin healing.

But when steroids are used long-term, the body stops producing its own cortisol.

And what happens when you suddenly stop?

The body goes into withdrawal.

The adrenal glands struggle to restart.

Inflammation comes back worse than before.

This was why I kept needing stronger and stronger steroids.

This was why my symptoms always came back the moment I stopped using them.

This was why my skin was now in a constant state of devastation.

This was never just eczema.

This was never just some chronic, unexplained condition.

This was addiction.

And the cure?

Stopping all steroids, forever.

I sat there, staring at the screen.

The words blurred together.

I read the same sentences over and over again, my brain refusing to accept what I was seeing.

This was it.

This was the answer I had been searching for.

But as the truth sank in, so did the fear.

I had been using steroids for years.

My body was completely dependent on them.

Every story I read about withdrawal was pure hell.

People described:

Burning skin.

Nerve pain.

Uncontrollable shedding.

Total body redness.

Oozing, insomnia, weight loss, months of being bedbound.

They weren't exaggerating.

This was real.

This was coming for me.

I wasn't just going to stop using steroids and magically heal.

I was about to go through the worst suffering of my life.

5:05. A Choice With No Easy Way Out

There were two options:

Option 1: Stay on steroids.

Continue cycling through stronger and stronger prescriptions.

Never fully heal, just mask the symptoms.

Eventually reach a point where even the strongest steroids wouldn't work anymore.

Accept a life of pain, dependency, and deteriorating health.

Option 2: Quit steroids forever.

Go through severe withdrawal.

Lose my ability to function for months, maybe even years.

Experience unimaginable pain, burning, and inflammation.

But, have a chance to heal for good.

This wasn't a real choice.
I knew what I had to do.
I had to quit.
I had to go through withdrawal.
I had to get my life back.

As terrifying as it was, there was no alternative.
I had been looking for an easy way out. A magic cure.
A treatment that would fix me without making things
worse first.
But there was no shortcut.
This was the only way.
I didn't know how bad it was going to get.
I didn't know if I was strong enough to survive it.
I didn't know if my life would ever be normal again.
But I did know one thing:
I wasn't going to let this ruin me.
I had made my decision.
And there was no turning back now.

The choice was made.
No more steroids.
No more false hope.

I was going cold turkey.
This wasn't just about stopping a medication.
This was about reclaiming my entire life.
I told myself:

"I can do this."

"I've already suffered for years, what's a few more months?"

"This is the only way out."

And maybe, just maybe...

I would finally get better.

But deep down?

I had no idea what was coming.

5:06. The Day That Changed Everything

March 14, 2015. The day I took back control.

Every single steroid cream, ointment, and tablet, gone.

No slow taper. No weaning off. Just straight-up, cold-turkey withdrawal.

For years, I had followed the system, trusting the doctors, believing that their solutions would eventually lead to relief. But relief never came, only more pain.

This was my last prescription. The last dose I would ever apply.

And that was it.

"Never again."

I had spent nearly five years suffering.

Five years of relentless pain.

Five years of discomfort, flares, and desperation.

So I told myself:

"How much worse can it get?"

"I already live with pain, what's a little more?"

"I've been through hell before. I can handle this."

I truly believed I was prepared.

109

I truly believed I understood suffering.
I truly believed this would be a short, painful phase before healing.
But I was wrong.
Not even close.
Because in hindsight, I now see,
I had no idea what was coming.
I had no idea what Topical Steroid Withdrawal (TSW) was about to do to me.
And within weeks, I would enter a nightmare unlike anything I had ever experienced before.

5:07. The First Few Days - False Hope

The moment I stopped using steroids, I felt ready.
I had read everything. I had convinced myself that no matter how bad it got, I could handle it.
For the first two days, nothing seemed too different.
The same discomfort.
The same itch.
The same burning cracks on my hands and feet.
"Maybe I won't have it as bad as others?"
"Maybe this whole withdrawal thing is exaggerated?"

Then, Day 3 came.
And I realised, I had no idea what I was about to face.
My hands and feet were more inflamed than ever, the skin felt tight, as if it was shrinking around my bones.
The itch was getting more intense.
The redness was spreading.

And then, it started moving up my wrists.

At first, I thought it was just irritation. Maybe the skin was reacting to being dry.

But then, my forearms started to itch.

Wait… why my forearms?

I hadn't put steroids there for years.

Yet the itch was relentless. It made no sense.

That was my first real lesson in Topical Steroid Withdrawal (TSW):

The damage isn't just where you applied the steroids.

Your entire body is withdrawing.

This wasn't just eczema.

This wasn't just a rash.

This was a full-body, systemic reaction.

And it was only just beginning.

5:08. Why Does Topical Steroid Withdrawal (TSW) Affect Areas That Were Never Treated?

At the time, I was completely confused, why were my forearms flaring? Why was my skin getting worse in places I had never put steroids?

Now, I know the answer:

Steroids don't just affect the skin, they suppress the entire body's natural cortisol production.

Cortisol is one of the body's most important hormones.

It controls:

Inflammation response

111

Immune function

Skin regeneration

Blood pressure

Stress response

when you use steroids over time, even if you only apply them to one area, your body becomes dependent on them to regulate inflammation.

The moment you stop, your body panics.

It doesn't remember how to regulate inflammation on its own. It overcompensates. It releases inflammatory chemicals uncontrollably.

That's why Topical Steroid Withdrawal (TSW) flares happen everywhere, because your entire system is reacting to the withdrawal.

I didn't know any of this at the time.

All I knew was that my skin was getting worse in places I had never expected.

5:09. Day 5 - The Red Mask Appears

It started with my face.

Red.

Deep, flushed redness, as if I had been standing under the sun for hours.

But I had never used steroids on my face.

That's when the fear crept in.

Why my face? At first, I told myself:

"Maybe I'm imagining it."

But then, it got darker.

Not just a little flushed, but a deep, unnatural redness that didn't fade.

It was a warning.

And I had no idea what was coming next.

By the end of the first week, I knew:

This was going to get worse. Much worse.

The burning, the redness, the itch, it was building.

I thought I had been prepared.

I thought I had already been through the worst of it.

I had no idea this was only the beginning.

5:10. Why Does Topical Steroid Withdrawal (TSW) Cause Extreme Redness?

At the time, I thought the redness was just part of the inflammation.

But now, I know the real reason:

Red Skin Syndrome (RSS) is a signature symptom of Topical Steroid Withdrawal (TSW).

When steroids are used for long periods, the blood vessels in the skin become permanently dilated.

Why?

Because steroids suppress inflammation by constricting blood vessels.

When you stop, the opposite happens, the blood vessels over-dilate.

This leads to:

Constant redness

Burning sensations

Intense heat radiating from the skin.

113

That's why Topical Steroid Withdrawal (TSW) skin often feels like it's on fire.

And by week one, I was already starting to feel that fire spreading.

I had no idea how bad it was about to get.

The real withdrawal hadn't even started yet.

My body was just warming up.

The real battle was about to begin.

And nothing could have prepared me for what came next.

5:11. The First Few Months - The Storm Begins

After the first week, everything started changing, day by day, hour by hour.

My body was shutting down.

My skin was falling apart.

I pushed through work for three weeks, three weeks of agony, forcing myself out of bed, pretending I was fine when every inch of me was screaming.

But then,

I couldn't do it anymore.

I had to stop.

I had read that Topical Steroid Withdrawal (TSW) spreads, but reading about it and experiencing it were two completely different things.

I could feel it happening.

Not just see it.

Not just react to it.

Feel it.

This wasn't a rash anymore.

It was a full-body invasion.

5:12. A Body Under Siege

The redness was relentless, starting on my hands and feet, then creeping up my wrists, my forearms, my legs. Within weeks, it was everywhere.

My arms, my back, my stomach, even places that had never had a single issue before, were now covered in inflammation.

Every morning, I woke up to new areas affected, skin that had been fine yesterday was suddenly burning, peeling, and raw.

And it wasn't just redness.

Deep cracks tore open across my hands, making even the lightest movement unbearable.

My feet were so damaged

Skin that should have been healing wasn't, it was stuck in a cycle of breaking, weeping, and drying into painful, hardened crusts.

My face, one of the last places I expected to suffer, was starting to swell.

It wasn't just puffiness.

My eyelids became so heavy that opening them was a struggle.

My lips felt thick and foreign, like I had been stung.

My entire face felt tight, stretched, like my skin didn't fit
my skull anymore. I had lost
Control of my own body.

5:13. The Worst Itch Imaginable

 I had experienced itching before.
Everyone has.
But this?
This was something else entirely.
This was an itch that didn't just live on the surface of my
skin,
it lived inside me.
It burrowed deep beneath the flesh, just out of reach.
It was relentless, cruel, never satisfied, never-ending.
 This wasn't a scratch and you're done kind of itch.
You chase it, but you never catch it.
The itch wasn't consistent, it was manipulative.
I scratched my arms, suddenly my legs were on fire.
I clawed at my legs, suddenly my back was screaming for
relief.
I ignored it, suddenly my face burned like I was standing
in flames.
Every time I tried to fight it, it moved, jumping from
place to place, laughing at me as I chased it in vain.
But I couldn't scratch properly.
Because my skin was already split, bleeding, and raw.
It was torture.

Pure, inescapable torture.
I could feel my nails digging into my flesh, but I couldn't stop.
I could hear the sound of my own skin tearing, but I kept going.
Because the relief was instant, but the regret was immediate.
The scratching didn't help.
But the need to scratch was stronger than my willpower.

5:14. No Sleep. No Escape

Nights were the worst.
I was already mentally drained, physically broken, but when the night came,
the itch became unbearable.
The burning intensified.
My body turned against me completely.
The moment I lay down,
the second my head touched the pillow,
it was like my skin went into full-blown attack mode.
I tried everything to stop it:
Positioning my arms differently, didn't help.
Wrapping my hands in bandages, still found ways to scratch.
Meditation techniques, pointless against something this powerful.
Nothing even came close to working.
I spent entire nights awake, in agony, my hands twitching,

and my mind screaming at me to just STOP
SCRATCHING.
But it was impossible.
This wasn't just a bad night's sleep.
This was nights on end with.

- Zero sleep.
- Zero rest.
- Zero peace.

I would lay there in the darkness, staring at the ceiling,
feeling trapped inside my own body.
Who even was I anymore?
Was this ever going to end?
I was fighting my own body,
but my body was winning.
Topical Steroid Withdrawal (TSW) wasn't just taking my
skin.
It was taking my sanity.
And I had no idea how much worse it was about to get.

5:15. The Suffering Spread to My Family

This wasn't just my suffering anymore.
The whole house was feeling the weight of it.
My wife was exhausted.
My kids could sense the tension.
The atmosphere at home had changed, it felt heavier.
This wasn't just about me anymore.

Ryan Thomson
The Eczema Deception

I wasn't the only one suffering, my family was suffering too.

My wife lay awake next to me, helpless, listening to me toss and turn, trying to hold back my scratching.

My kids saw their dad change, once strong, full of life, now a shadow of himself.

My home, once filled with laughter, warmth, and love, felt like a battleground.

I was losing everything, not just my skin.

I was losing my sense of self-worth.

And worst of all, I didn't know when it would end.

Left photo was the first noticeable change in my face, then the swelling started. These are just 5 days apart.

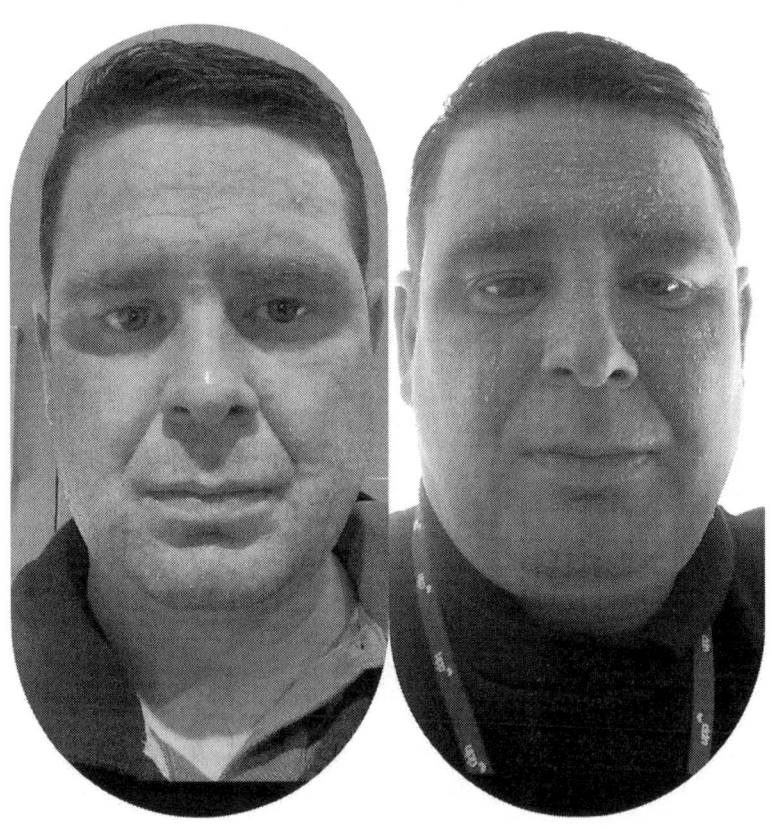

The face continued to get dryer and split and was
like this for many months

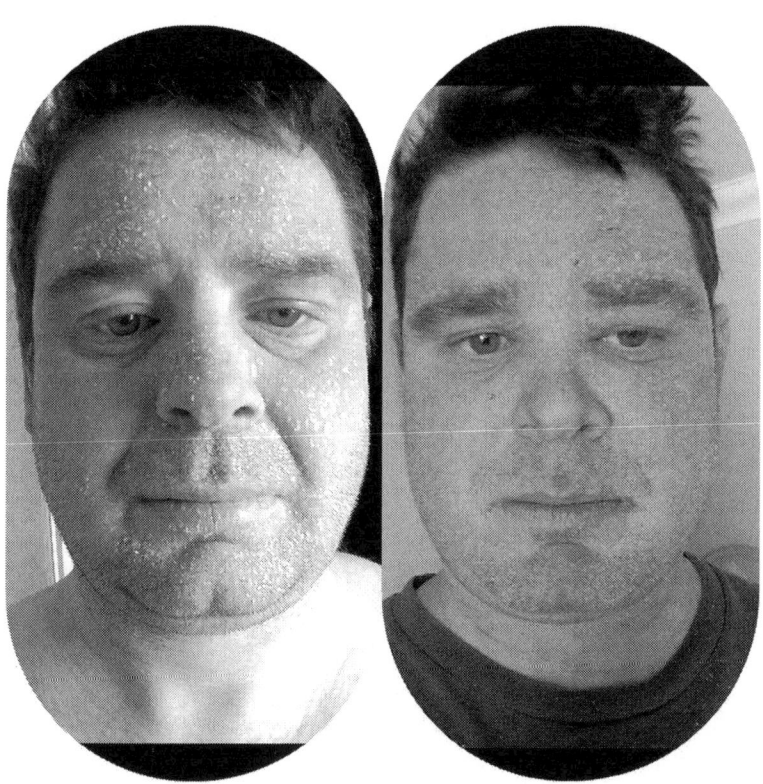

5:16. The Treatments That Helped (And What Didn't)

In the midst of the chaos, I was desperate for any kind of relief.
I knew there was no cure, no magic pill, no instant fix.
But I needed something. Anything.
Some treatments helped in small ways, even if just for a moment.
Others? A complete waste of time.
So, here's what worked for me, and what didn't.

Sudocrem - A Thick Barrier for Broken Skin.
What is it?
A zinc oxide-based cream originally used for nappy rash, burns, and pressure sores.

Why did I use it?
Because my skin was so raw, open, and exposed, I needed something to create a barrier, something to protect the deep cracks and open wounds.

How it helped:
Created a strong protective layer over open skin
Reduced irritation and acted as a mild numbing agent
Helped with weeping areas by drying them out slightly

What it didn't do:
Didn't heal the skin, only protected it

Was messy as hell, stained clothes, bedsheets, and left a

white film everywhere

Would I recommend it:
Yes, for small areas where the skin is cracked or bleeding.
But for large areas? Too thick, too uncomfortable.

Cetraben - A Lifesaver for Dry Skin

What is it?
A paraffin-based emollient designed for eczema and
chronic dry skin conditions.
Why did I use it?
Because most moisturisers burned like hell, but I still
needed to combat the extreme dryness that came with
Topical Steroid Withdrawal (TSW).
How it helped:

Didn't sting on application, which was rare for a
moisturiser
Absorbed quickly without feeling greasy.
Gave temporary relief from the tight, dry feeling

What it didn't do:
Didn't stop the itch, only soothed the dryness.
Didn't prevent flaking or cracking, just softened the skin
for a while.

Would I recommend it?
Yes, but with caution.

Moisturisers are hit or miss for people going through
Topical Steroid Withdrawal (TSW).
Some find they make things worse (called moisture
withdrawal) - so it's all about trial and error.

 Coconut Oil - The Overhyped Solution
why did I try it?
Because so many people online swore by it, saying it was
a miracle for inflammation, itching, and dry skin.

How it helped:
Felt cooling on application, at first

Why I stopped using it:
Made my skin itch more, felt like it triggered a reaction

Left a greasy film that didn't absorb well

Offered zero long-term relief

Would I recommend it?
Honestly? No.
It might work for some, but for me, it just made things
worse.

 Epsom Salt Baths - The Greatest Relief of All.
This was my biggest saviour.

What are they?
Epsom salts (magnesium sulphate crystals) dissolve in

water and are known for their skin-soothing and anti-inflammatory benefits.

How it helped:
Instantly calmed the burning itch

Loosened up stiff, cracked skin

Reduced inflammation for a short time

Made my hands feel normal again, while I was in the bath

The downside:
Relief only lasted while I was in the water

Coming out of the bath was brutal, the skin tightened back up fast

Would I recommend it?
100% YES.
Even though the relief was temporary, it was worth it just to have those few moments of peace.

At the end of the day?
Nothing truly worked.
There was no miracle cream, no special oil, and no hidden cure.
Some things soothed the pain for a while,
but nothing stopped the process.
Because the truth was simple but brutal:
The only way out was through.

5:17. Surviving the First Months - The Reality

I wasn't healing yet.

I was just surviving.

Every day was a new challenge, a constant battle against my own body.

Days became unbearable. There was no relief, no break, and no escape.

By this point, I was completely unrecognisable.

My face had transformed, swollen beyond recognition, the skin stretched tight and inflamed. Every facial movement, smiling, speaking, even blinking, caused tiny fissures to form, ripping my skin apart.

My body was raw, coated in scabs, oozing patches, and dry crusts that peeled away in chunks, only to be replaced with more inflamed, broken skin.

Every touch, every movement hurt. Clothes rubbing against me felt like sandpaper on a fresh wound. The air itself stung.

My body was shutting down.

But the worst of it wasn't the pain.

It was the itch.

This was something beyond human comprehension.

Why was the itch so unbearable?

This was nerve-deep. It was systemic. It wasn't just my skin reacting, it was my entire nervous system going haywire.

It was driven by withdrawal. My body was no longer

receiving the artificial cortisol it had been dependent on for years, sending it into a state of shock.

The Science behind It:

When you stop using steroids, your body suddenly loses its external source of cortisol.

Cortisol isn't just an anti-inflammatory, it helps regulate immune responses, nerve signaling, and the skin barrier.

Without it, the body overreacts:

The immune system goes into a frenzy, triggering massive inflammation.

The nerves become hypersensitive, sending constant false signals of irritation and pain.

The skin barrier is compromised, leaving me completely exposed to external irritants, temperature changes, and even my own sweat.

The result?

A full-body sensory overload.

The itch wasn't just an itch; it was a neurological malfunction.

5:18. A Battle I Could Never Win

I was trapped in my own body, and I had no idea how much longer this was going to last.

I used to think I understood exhaustion.

I'd worked long shifts before, back-to-back days on-site, grinding through the fatigue. I'd pulled all-nighters as an electrician, finishing jobs that had to be done before the deadline.

I knew what it felt like to push through the dragging

weight of sleep deprivation.

But this?

This wasn't exhaustion.

This was something else. Something darker.

As soon as the sky started to dim, the dread would creep in.

Another night.

Another battle.

Another eight-hour war I was guaranteed to lose.

I would go to bed knowing exactly what was coming.

Knowing that, yet again, I was going to spend the entire night trapped in a cycle of itching, burning, and suffering.

And yet, I still hoped.

Hoped that maybe, just maybe, tonight would be different.

But the second my head hit the pillow, the itch took over.

The burning intensified, like my skin was trying to suffocate me from the inside out.

The deep, bone-level itch pulsed beneath the surface, impossible to reach, impossible to ignore.

The sensation crawled across my body, arms, legs, chest, neck, never settling, never stopping.

I would flip from one side to the other, trying to find a position that didn't make my skin scream,

I would shift, adjust, stretch, and curl up, anything to calm the unbearable sensation.

Then the hours would start slipping away.

Midnight.

1 AM.

2 AM.

3 AM.

Still lying there. Still wide awake.

Still scratching. Still burning. Still suffering.

My wife was asleep beside me, peacefully resting, while I was trapped in my own personal hell.

By 4 AM, I couldn't take it anymore.

I'd get up.

I'd pace the house.

I'd drag my mangled feet across the floor, leaving a trail of skin behind me.

I tried everything.

Maybe a cup of tea will help.

Maybe watching TV will distract me.

Maybe just closing my eyes and breathing will do something.

Nothing ever worked.

5:19. Morning Came, and I Was Still Awake

By 5 AM, the first light of morning crept through the window.

A new day had begun.

And I hadn't slept a single second.

Then, the world around me started to wake up.

The smell of coffee brewing in the kitchen.

The sound of little feet padding across the floor.

The hum of the shower running.

Life was beginning again.

For everyone else, it was a fresh start.

For me?

It was just another reminder that I had made it through another night in hell, only to do it all over again.

I used to be the first one up.

The one getting ready for work, grabbing a quick coffee, rushing out the door.

The one driving the kids to school, chatting about their day ahead, making them laugh.

The one my wife could depend on, the man who kept everything running.

But now?

Now, I was just there.

A useless, flaking, swollen mess.

I wasn't a husband.

I wasn't a father.

I wasn't a provider.

I was just a shell.

Every morning, I sat there watching life move forward, while I was stuck in place.

Would I ever be me again?

Would I ever be the man they needed?

Or was this all I was now?

A sick, useless man who couldn't even hug his own kids without his skin breaking apart.

A man who was fading away right in front of them.

5:20. The Endless Cycle - Three Nights Awake, Then a Crash

This cycle continued for months.

Three full nights awake.

Three days of suffering, no sleep, no rest, just burning, itching, and mental torture.

Then on the fourth day, my body would finally give in.

I'd pass out, not in my bed, but on the sofa, or wherever I collapsed from exhaustion.

A couple of hours of unconsciousness, not sleep, just my body shutting down.

Then the cycle would start all over again.

It was inhumane.

It was never-ending.

And worst of all?

There was no drug strong enough to overpower it.

I tried everything.

Sleeping pills? Nothing. Like taking a Tic Tac.

Night Nurse? Pointless.

Antihistamines? May as well have taken sugar pills.

Over-the-counter sleep aids? A joke.

The medical system had no answers for this.

Because this wasn't normal insomnia.

This was my nervous system being fried by withdrawal.

This was my body screaming at me for stopping steroids.

This was my brain trapped in a cycle of stress, inflammation, and survival mode.

I wasn't just losing sleep.

I was losing my sanity.

5:21. The Sleep Strategies I Wish I Had Known

Looking back, I've learned that while nothing completely stopped the insomnia, there were some things that could have lessened the suffering.
If I could go back and tell myself how to get through those nights, these are the things I would say:

1. Magnesium for Sleep & Nervous System Support
Magnesium glycinate or magnesium L-threonate can help calm the nervous system and promote deeper sleep.
Many people with Topical Steroid Withdrawal (TSW) are deficient in magnesium, which is essential for relaxing muscles, reducing stress, and aiding sleep.
What to try:
- Take magnesium glycinate before bed.
- Magnesium spray or baths can also help relax the skin and muscles.

2. The Ice Pack Trick - Cooling the Itch
Heat worsens itching and inflammation. Cooling the skin can calm the nervous system and slow the itch response.
What to try:

Wrap an ice pack in a towel and rest it on the worst areas before bed
Keep a bowl of cold water next to your bed to dip your hands in when the itching gets too intense.

Try cooling gel packs for longer relief.

3. White Noise & Sleep Hypnosis
Topical Steroid Withdrawal (TSW) overstimulates the nervous system. Sound therapy can help distract the brain from the itch and slow racing thoughts.
What to try:

White noise machines or apps to drown out discomfort.
Sleep hypnosis tracks - proven to slow brainwave activity and ease the body into a sleep state.
Brown noise - deeper and more soothing than white noise, known for helping with insomnia.

4. CBD & Herbal Remedies
CBD oil can help regulate the nervous system and promote sleep.
 Herbal teas like chamomile, valerian root, and passionflower can help relax the body.
What to try:

CBD oil under the tongue 30 minutes before bed.
A strong chamomile & valerian tea to drink an hour before sleep.
Lavender essential oil on your pillow or in a diffuser.

5. Sleep Hygiene - Rewiring the Brain for Rest.
The brain needs routines to know when to shut down.
Topical Steroid Withdrawal (TSW) destroys sleep cycles, but these habits can help reset them:
What to try:

Dim the lights 2 hours before bed - artificial light tricks the brain into staying awake.

Set a "wind-down" routine - do the same relaxing things every night.

Keep the room cool - lower temperatures signal the body to sleep.

5:22. How Weed Helped Me Survive

I don't know how much worse it would have been if I hadn't discovered weed.

It wasn't a cure.

It didn't fix my skin.

It didn't magically make Topical Steroid Withdrawal (TSW) disappear.

But it saved my sanity.

When I smoked weed, I felt a little calmer.

It took the edge off the anxiety.

It gave me a brief moment of peace.

The itch was still there.

The pain was still there.

But something about it softened the mental toll.

Weed didn't stop the suffering, but it made it a fraction more bearable.

And in Topical Steroid Withdrawal (TSW)?

Sometimes, that's all you need to keep going.

The Medical Benefits of Weed for Topical Steroid Withdrawal (TSW) & Insomnia

The medical world is finally catching up to something sufferers have known for years, cannabis has real therapeutic effects for people dealing with chronic pain, inflammation, and sleep disorders.

For Topical Steroid Withdrawal (TSW) sufferers, it can help in several ways:

Reduces Anxiety - Chronic sleep deprivation and pain spike cortisol levels, the body's stress hormone. Cannabis helps lower anxiety and promote relaxation.

Calms the Nervous System - Topical Steroid Withdrawal (TSW) causes overactive nerves, constant itching, and burning. Cannabis has been shown to soothe nerve pain and inflammation.

Mild Pain Relief - It doesn't erase pain, but it dulls the sharpest edges of the suffering.

Appetite Stimulation - Topical Steroid Withdrawal (TSW) makes eating difficult due to stress and nausea. Cannabis can help regulate appetite and encourage eating when the body is in distress.

Induces Drowsiness - THC, the psychoactive compound in cannabis, binds to sleep receptors in the brain, helping regulate sleep cycles.

Is It for Everyone?

I'm not saying weed is the answer for everyone.

I'm not saying it's a magic bullet.

I'm not even saying its right for you.

But for me?

It helped me survive.

135

It gave me moments of peace when nothing else could. And in the absolute worst of my withdrawal, that was enough.

5:23. Surviving on Empty

By the third month, I wasn't even existing anymore, I was just enduring.

Sleep was a distant memory.

Pain had become my only companion.

Every single day felt like a slow-motion nightmare.

I had no concept of time anymore. The days blurred into one long, agonising loop.

Wake up. (If I had slept at all.)

Try to function. (Fail.)

Try to distract myself. (Fail.)

Try not to scratch. (Fail.)

This wasn't just a skin condition.

This wasn't just a phase that would pass.

This was Topical Steroid Withdrawal.

And it had stolen everything from me.

5:24. The Redness, The Swelling, and The Horror of Oozing Skin

I had read about Red Skin Syndrome, but now?
I was living it.

At first, the redness crept in slowly, a faint flush, like my skin was irritated.

Then, almost overnight, it was like my entire body had been set on fire.

The redness deepened, darkened, spread like an infection taking over my skin.

My reflection in the mirror became unrecognisable, blotchy, raw, angry.

The heat coming off my body was unreal, I felt like I was radiating fire.

I watched as my skin turned redder by the hour.

Not just a rash, this was a full-body reaction.

It felt like my blood itself was burning me from the inside out.

I begged for the heat to stop.

I tried cold compresses.

I tried standing in front of a fan.

I tried splashing cold water on my face.

Nothing worked.

It was as if my entire immune system had gone into meltdown.

But the worst part?

The redness wasn't just skin-deep.

I could feel it, deep inside, pulsing, throbbing, raging.

Like my skin was suffocating from the inside out.

Then came the swelling.

And that's when I truly lost control.

Edema - The Swelling That Transformed Me into a Monster

At first, I barely noticed it.
Maybe I'm just retaining a bit of water?
Maybe I haven't been moving around enough?
Maybe this is normal?
But my body was ballooning out of control.
My skin stretched tighter and tighter.
My limbs felt like they didn't belong to me.
I could physically feel the pressure building inside my own body.
Something was very, very wrong.
Why Was This Happening?

Edema is the body's desperate attempt to hold onto fluid when something is drastically wrong.
And in Topical Steroid Withdrawal (TSW), the body is in complete shutdown mode.
My blood vessels were leaking fluid into my skin.
My lymphatic system, designed to drain excess fluid, was failing.
My body had completely lost control of regulating itself.
It wasn't just swelling.
It was my body drowning in its own fluids.

5:25. Losing Control of My Own Body

I watched in horror as my body inflated before my eyes.
My feet doubled in size. They looked like they belonged to someone twice my weight.
My ankles completely disappeared. I no longer had ankles, just puffy, fluid-filled masses of flesh.

Ryan Thomson
The Eczema Deception

My hands were so swollen I could barely bend my fingers.

Every step was agony.

The swelling pressed against my nerves, making my legs feel like they were going to burst.

My hands throbbed with a constant, unbearable pressure.

Even my eyelids swelled, making my face look distorted and unrecognisable.

Shoes? Forget it.

Socks? Left painful, deep indents in my skin.

Walking? Every step felt like I was carrying an extra 50 pounds of dead weight.

I had to buy Crocs.

Two sizes too big.

The only thing I could squeeze my swollen, bloated feet into.

And I hated it.

I had never worn Crocs in my life.

I used to think they were ridiculous.

But now?

I didn't care about fashion.

I didn't care about looking good.

I didn't care about anything anymore.

I was unrecognisable.

Every time I looked in the mirror, a stranger stared back at me.

A monster, bloated, swollen, deformed.

And then,

The oozing started.

One morning, I was glued to my sheets.

Not because of sweat.

Not because of moisture.

But because of the thick, yellow, oozing fluid leaking from my skin.

This was not normal sweat.

This was not just water.

This was my body breaking down.

I reached for my top, only to realise it was stuck to me.

I peeled it off slowly, and as the fabric tore away, so did my skin.

A thin layer of flesh came off with it, leaving behind glistening, raw, open wounds.

My arms shone under the light, not with moisture, but with a continuous flow of leaking fluid.

Every movement pulled my skin apart, stretching and tearing the fragile, sticky, cracked surface.

This wasn't sweat.

This wasn't infection.

This was my lymphatic fluid, leaking from my body, as if my skin could no longer hold itself together.

I wasn't just losing my skin.

I was losing my body's ability to function.

The ooze would seep out in thick, slow-moving droplets.

Then, it would dry and harden, forming a brittle yellow shell over my raw skin.

Then, the shell would crack, exposing even more of my damaged flesh.

And the cycle would repeat.

Every. Single. Day.

Every morning, I had to peel my clothes off my skin like tearing off an old, stubborn bandage.

Ryan Thomson
The Eczema Deception

It hurt like hell.

And then there was the smell.

There are no words to describe it.

Not rotten.

Not sour.

Not like infection.

It was metallic.

A sharp, chemical-like, almost blood-tinged scent that clung to everything.

No amount of washing got rid of it.

No soap, no scrub, no detergent could mask it.

I could smell myself even when I wasn't moving.

It was like my body was purging something unnatural.

Like it was desperately trying to rid itself of poison.

And as my skin continued to ooze, swell, and crack apart, I realised something terrifying.

This was only getting worse.

The red burning itchy rash on the legs and the swelling starting.

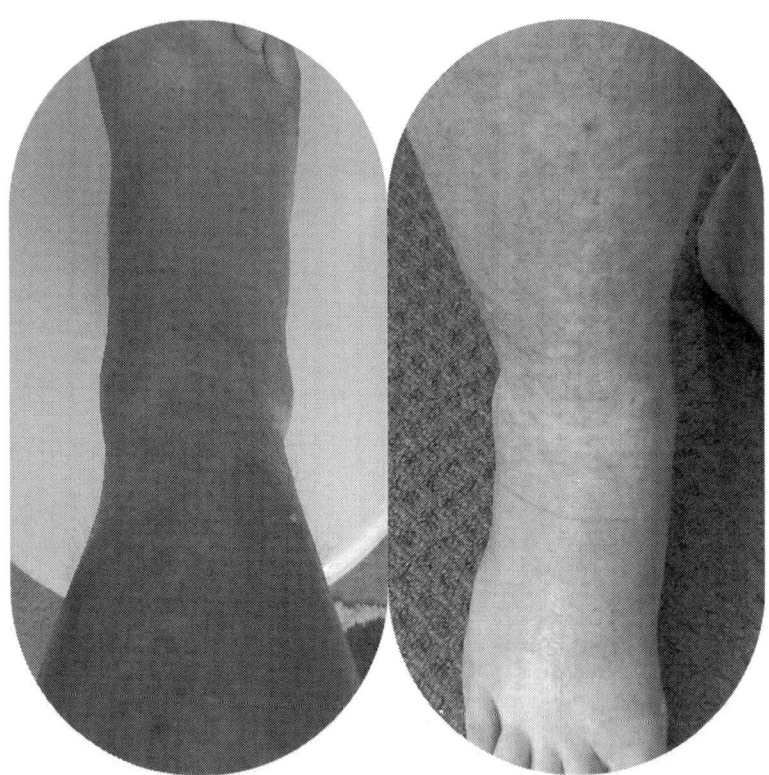

The swelling continued to get worse and remained like this until the end of my stay in guys when I 1st noticed the swelling start to go down

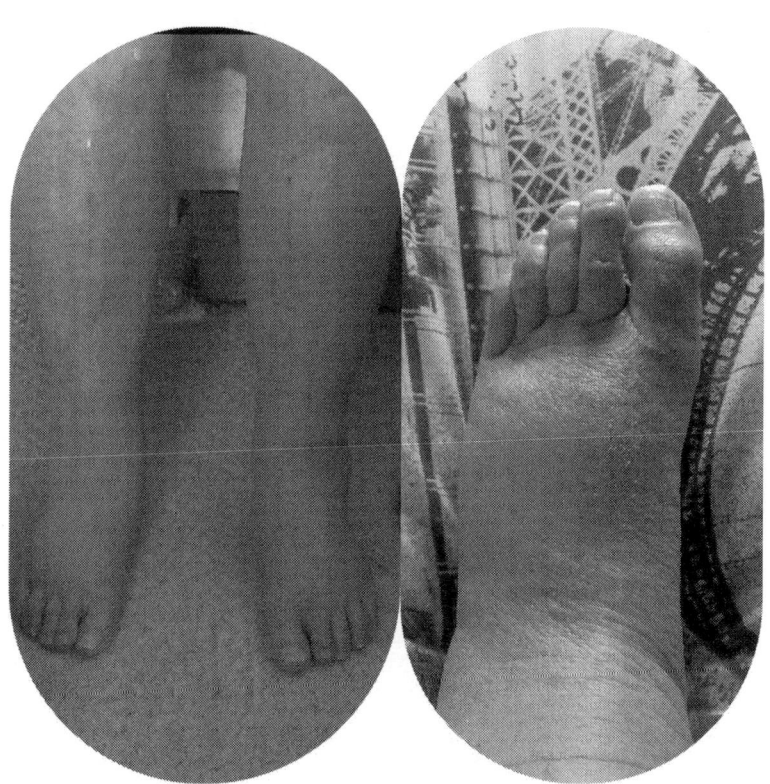

My ankle was left with this dryness and deep splits
the pain was excruciating.

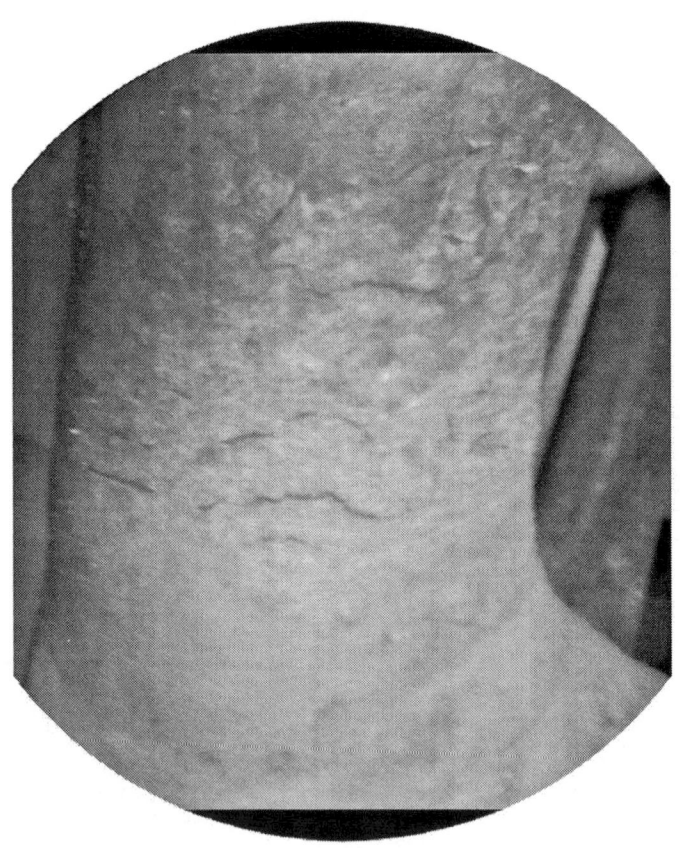

5:26. The Doubt and the Fear - Had I Made the Biggest Mistake of My Life?

The questions wouldn't stop.

Had I done the right thing?

Or had I completely destroyed myself?

Was Topical Steroid Withdrawal (TSW) real? Or was I just refusing to accept that I had a real condition?

I had spent years being told that steroids were my only option.

Now, without them, I was in the worst state of my life.

My skin was falling apart.

My body was unrecognisable.

My mind was breaking.

How could this be right?

Everything I had ever learned told me that doctors knew best.

They had studied for years.

They had experience with thousands of patients.

They had seen conditions like mine before, hadn't they?

But if they were right,

Why was I getting worse?

Why had every treatment failed me?

Why did I only find relief when I stopped listening to them?

I didn't know what to believe anymore.

I didn't know who was right.

I didn't even recognise myself.

I had too much time to think.

Days without sleep.

Nights dragging on forever.

Hours and hours trapped in my own head.

The fear was real.

What if I was wrong?

What if I was actually sick and refusing treatment?

What if this wasn't withdrawal, but something worse?

What if I was dying?

Because this didn't feel like healing.

This felt like pure, slow, unbearable destruction.

I had walked into this thinking I was choosing freedom.

Instead, I had chosen suffering beyond belief.

And for the first time, I wondered,

Had I made the biggest mistake of my life?

5:27. Battling the Dermatologists - A War I Fought Alone

By the time my next dermatology appointment at Canterbury Hospital came around, I was deep into Topical Steroid Withdrawal (TSW) hell.

Every step into that clinic felt like dragging chains behind me.

The fluourescent lights were harsh against my already burning skin, and I could feel the stares before I even sat down.

For years, I had walked into these rooms with the same problems, blistered hands, cracked feet, unbearable itching.

But this time?

I was unrecognisable.

They had been monitoring my hands and feet for years.

146

Now, my entire body was covered in red, inflamed, cracked, swollen, and oozing skin.

Now, I looked like a severe burn victim.

I could see it in their eyes the moment they looked at me, the shock. The confusion. The quiet horror.

They didn't even try to hide it.

"What have you done?"

"Why did you stop the steroids?"

"This is dangerous."

It wasn't concern.

It wasn't care.

It was disapproval.

They weren't worried about me. They were frustrated.

Frustrated that I had gone against their system.

Frustrated because now, they had no clue what to do with me.

The conversation escalated quickly.

Here I was, an electrician, standing my ground against medical professionals who had studied for years.

Telling them that I knew better than them.

And they thought I was insane.

From their perspective, I looked 100 times worse than before.

From my perspective, I was finally seeing the real cause of my suffering.

"Ryan, you need to go back on steroids. This isn't safe."

No.

"We can do a controlled course, taper you off properly this time."

No.

"You're making yourself suffer for nothing."

NO.

I wasn't going through this living hell just to end up back at square one.

"How many times have you prescribed me steroids, and how many times have I come back worse than before?"

"How many drugs have you tried on me, and how many have failed?"

"Tell me, after five years, has ANYTHING you prescribed actually fixed me?"

Silence.

They couldn't answer.

Because they knew the truth just as well as I did.

At this point, it didn't feel like I was sitting across from doctors.

It felt like I was sitting across from drug dealers.

They couldn't accept that their treatment had caused this.

They wouldn't accept that I had taken control of my own health.

Instead, they just kept pushing the steroids.

"Just a short course to get you back on track."

"We can use them carefully this time."

"We'll monitor you closely."

I had heard it all before.

I wasn't falling for it again.

"No. I'm done with steroids."

They kept trying.

They couldn't comprehend that I was rejecting the only tool they knew how to use.

But I wasn't their usual patient.

I wasn't just someone who followed instructions blindly.

I wasn't part of their system anymore.

I was defying them.

And they had no clue what to do with me.

Since I refused steroids, they had nothing left
to offer me.

The only thing they could do?

More Cetraben, which I was already getting through at an insane rate.

And a new cream, Psoriderm.

But at this point, I had lost all faith in them.

I knew that whatever they gave me was just another
attempt to control symptoms, never to cure the root
cause.

And for the first time since this nightmare began, I
walked out of that hospital knowing I was on my own.

Psoriderm - The Thick, Sticky, Stinking Nightmare
Psoriderm was unlike anything I had ever used before.

The smell hit me like a punch to the face.

A thick, suffocating stench of coal tar, chemical-heavy,
lingering in the air long after the lid was closed.

It clung to my skin, clothes, and bedsheets, permeating
everything in its path.

I walked through the house, and my wife would wrinkle
her nose before I even said a word.

"Jesus, Ryan, what the hell is that smell?"

It was me.

I was the smell.

And no matter how many times I washed my hands,
scrubbed my skin, or aired out my room,

It. Would. Not. Go. Away.

I kept using it out of desperation.

Until I finally realised, it wasn't helping at all.

I threw the Psoriderm in the bin.

I'd rather suffer through Topical Steroid Withdrawal (TSW) naturally than coat myself in that disgusting sludge ever again.

5:28. They Had No Answers, So They Passed Me On

I had been under Canterbury Hospital's dermatology team for years.

They had prescribed me everything under the sun.

They had run every test imaginable.

And now?

They were done with me.

At my next appointment, I could feel it the moment I walked into the room.

The energy was different.

The enthusiasm was gone.

They didn't even pretend to be hopeful anymore.

They had given up.

"There's nothing more we can do for you."

"We've tried every treatment available."

"You need to be referred to a specialist centre."

I wasn't a patient to them anymore,

I was a problem to be handed off.

Since I had refused steroids, they had no idea what to do with me.

A rebel patient.

A difficult case.

Someone who wasn't listening to their 'expert' advice.

"If you won't take steroids, then there's nothing more we can offer you."

"We're going to transfer you to London's Guy's Hospital Dermatology Department."
Why Guy's Hospital?
For years, I had been treated like just another eczema case.
Now? I was a complex case.
Guy's Hospital in London has one of the top dermatology units in the country.
It's where they send the patients they don't know how to fix.
If they couldn't help me, who could?
I had mixed emotions.
On one hand:
Maybe this was a good thing.
Maybe the specialists in London would finally understand Topical Steroid Withdrawal (TSW).
Maybe I would get real help.
But on the other hand:
What if they just pushed steroids again?
What if they had no idea what Topical Steroid Withdrawal (TSW) was?
What if I was wasting my time chasing another dead end?
I didn't know what to think.
I didn't know if I should feel hopeful or defeated.
But one thing was clear,
Canterbury Hospital had washed their hands of me.
I was no longer their problem.
And now, my fate was in the hands of Guy's Hospital.

5:29. The Mental Battle

Topical Steroid Withdrawal was a war unlike anything I
had ever faced.

But if I had to pinpoint what broke me the most,
it wasn't just the pain, the sleepless nights, the endless
itch, or the way my body was falling apart.
It was the mental torment.
Topical Steroid Withdrawal (TSW) didn't just strip away
my skin,
it stripped away my identity, my purpose, my dignity.
I wasn't just fighting to survive physically.
I was fighting to stay sane.
I was never an angry person. Frustrated at times, sure,
but never full of rage. Yet, over the years, this ordeal had
changed me. I was angry, angry at what they had done to
me, angry at how this had stripped me of everything I
once was. I was angry that I could no longer support my
family the way I had always done, angry that I was losing
everything and everyone close to me.
I felt hopeless. Alone. Isolated. And yet, I was in a house
full of people.
The anger seeped into everyday moments. I would catch
myself snapping at those around me, my patience worn
down to nothing. That wasn't me. At least, it never used
to be. But now, apparently, this was who I had become. I
don't think I was easy to be around, I probably wasn't
pleasant at all. But how could I be? I was suffering in
ways I had never suffered before, physically, mentally,
emotionally.
Even basic hygiene was a struggle. Running water over

my hands felt like needles piercing my skin. Every wash, every touch, was agony. But there was one thing that brought me even the slightest relief, my Epsom salt baths. Twice a day, I would soak in warm water infused with Epsom salts and tea tree oil, the only moments where I felt somewhat normal. Lying there, staring at the ceiling, lost in my own thoughts, those baths became my only escape. The only part of my day that didn't feel like pure suffering.

And for months, that was the highlight of my life.

Money was running out.

My wife took on foreign exchange students in our spare room, helping bring in extra money when my earnings dropped.

I was grateful.

But I hated it.

I was supposed to be the one providing.

I was supposed to be the strong one.

I looked around my home and saw all the unfinished projects I had started.

The patio in the garden, half-done.

The DIY tasks I had once loved, abandoned.

I didn't just feel useless.

I felt like a failure.

It wasn't just me suffering.

Topical Steroid Withdrawal (TSW) was affecting my entire family.

And I could feel it.

The atmosphere in the house changed.

The laughter was gone.

The excitement was gone.

The normality was gone.

Instead, my wife had another child to look after,

Me.

She was already raising our kids.

Now she was also:

Cleaning up my flaking skin wherever I went.

Washing my blood-stained, ooze-covered clothes and bedsheets.

Listening to my constant complaints about pain, discomfort, and itching.

The strain on her was unbearable.

And intimacy?

Gone.

Who would want to touch a body covered in open wounds, flakes, and ooze?

Who would find this attractive?

How could I ever feel wanted again?

Topical Steroid Withdrawal (TSW) robbed us of everything.

We were running out of money.

We had no savings.

We had no backup plan.

So we made the hardest decision.

We had to sell our rental house.

That property was my pension fund.

The only safety net we had for the future.

Now?

We had no choice but to sell it just to survive.

Topical Steroid Withdrawal (TSW) didn't just take my skin.

It took my life.

And the scariest part?

There was no cure.

No end date.

No way to know when this suffering would stop.

I was fighting a war I never signed up for.

"But the war wasn't just physical, it was mental. And as my body crumbled, so did my mind.

That was a battle I never expected to lose."

Just when it felt like everything was slipping through our fingers, one of my best friends, Mark Weatherall, stepped in. We had been friends for over thirty years by that point, and his generosity during this time was something I will never forget. Mark offered to lend us some money to keep us afloat for a few months until the sale of our rental house went through. That financial support made an immense difference, I genuinely don't know how we would have survived without it.

But Mark didn't just help financially, he, along with a few other close friends, chipped in to help finish the patio as well. I was in no state to do much, but I managed to just about make tea for them as they worked away, transforming the unfinished space into something we could actually use. It wasn't just a home improvement project; it was a gift. A better garden for the kids to play in, a proper place to sit outside, and a reminder that even in the darkest times, good friends will step up when you need them the most.

That act of kindness stayed with me. It was a reminder that, no matter how much Topical Steroid Withdrawal (TSW) had taken from me, there were still people who cared, people who wanted to help, and people who refused to let me drown in this nightmare alone.

Chapter 6. Guy's Hospital

6:01. The Journey to Guy's Hospital

The day of my first appointment at Guy's Hospital had arrived, a milestone I faced with a mix of apprehension and resignation. My faith in the medical system had been severely shaken, and the prospect of advocating for myself regarding Topical Steroid Withdrawal (TSW) felt daunting.

Would they listen?

Would they dismiss me like the others had?

Would this trip be worth it?

My dad accompanied me, offering his support for the journey ahead.

Residing in Canterbury, the trip to London was both a logistical challenge and a financial burden.

Cost of travel:

Peak time fare: £78

Off-peak fare: £40

For a family already struggling financially, these journeys weren't just exhausting, they were crippling.

The hour-long high-speed train ride to London St Pancras was followed by a transfer to the Northern Line, leading us to London Bridge, where Guy's Hospital is situated.

At approximately two and a half months into Topical

Steroid Withdrawal (TSW), my condition had reached a critical point.

My skin was a patchwork of raw, inflamed areas interspersed with peeling flakes.

The incessant itching and burning sensations were relentless.

Every movement reminded me of my fragility, the simple act of clothing brushing against my skin could trigger waves of pain.

6:02. The Train Ride - A Journey of Discomfort

As we boarded the train, I became aware of the stares from fellow passengers.

Their eyes lingered on my visibly distressed skin.

I could sense their discomfort.

I felt like an oddity on display.

Each glance amplified my sense of isolation.

The train's vibrations made it worse, intensifying the burning sensation that coursed through my body.

Every jolt of movement sent fresh stabs of pain through my skin.

By the time we arrived at London Bridge, I was already exhausted.

The bustling atmosphere was overwhelming.

Honking horns.
Distant sirens.
Crowds of commuters brushing past.
Every accidental brush against another person sent jolts
of pain through my hypersensitive skin.
Approaching Guy's Hospital, its towering structure
loomed above, both imposing and intimidating.
The modern architecture, sleek lines, and glass facades
felt cold and unwelcoming.
The sterile scent of the hospital hit me the moment we
stepped inside.
The bright lighting, polished floors, and clinical ambiance
only added to my sense of dread.

6:03. The Waiting Room - A Familiar Feeling of Isolation

We navigated through corridors until we reached the
Southwark Wing and ascended to the third floor.
The waiting area was modest,
Rows of chairs lined up in a utilitarian fashion.
Muted wall tones, intended to be calming, but instead
feeling impersonal.
A television playing daytime programs with subtitles.
There was no music, just the occasional intercom
announcement and the soft murmur of conversations.
I glanced at my dad.
He nodded at me, as if reassuring me.
But the uncertainty weighed heavily in the air.

Would these doctors be any different?
Or was I in for another battle?

6:04. Facing the Doctors at Guy's Hospital

I had been here before.
A hospital waiting room. A dermatology appointment. A discussion I already knew too well.
Only this time, I was prepared for a fight.
After what felt like an eternity, my name was called.
I stood up, my dad by my side, and followed the doctor into the consultation room.
A Different Atmosphere
The setup here was different from Canterbury.
More modern.
More welcoming.
Less dismissive, at least at first.
It gave me a glimmer of hope that maybe, just maybe, this appointment might be different.
The doctor, with a reassuring smile, glanced over my medical history before looking up and saying,
"Tell me about your journey, in your own words."
I took a deep breath and laid it all out:
1. The Initial Spot - The small, seemingly harmless rash that started it all.
2. Progression of Symptoms - How my condition spiraled out of control despite following medical advice.
3. Treatments Taken - Every cream, tablet, and immunosuppressant I had been given, and how they all failed me.

4. The Impact on My Life - How my skin had robbed me of my job, my sleep, my ability to function.

5. Discovering Topical Steroid Withdrawal (TSW) - The video, the research, and my realisation that steroids were the cause of my suffering.

6. My Battles with Canterbury Hospital - The dismissive doctors, the arguments, the refusal to acknowledge Topical Steroid Withdrawal (TSW).

I was tired of being dismissed.

I needed them to listen.

I needed them to believe me.

The doctor listened intently, her expression thoughtful.

She didn't interrupt.

She didn't dismiss me outright.

She let me finish.

For the first time in years, I felt like a doctor was actually hearing me.

6:05. The Examination & The Treatment Plan

After my account, she conducted a thorough examination.

She acknowledged my concerns but suggested a short course of steroids to calm the flare-up.

Here we go again!!

"No."

"I won't use steroids. Not again."

She respected my decision.

Instead, she outlined a non-steroidal treatment plan:

Blood tests to rule out any underlying conditions.

50/50 ointment (white soft paraffin + liquid paraffin) to act as a moisture barrier.

Follow-up appointment scheduled for the next week.

For the first time in a long time, I felt heard.

The dreaded steroid conversation was behind me.

Dad suggested we take a detour to Borough Market, knowing how much I loved the place.

The smell of fresh bread.

The sight of artisan cheeses.

The sizzling of street food.

For a moment, I felt normal.

For a moment, I wasn't just a Topical Steroid Withdrawal (TSW) sufferer.

For a moment, I was me.

As we made our way back home, I reflected on the day.

The journey had been exhausting.

The train fare was a financial strain.

The fight wasn't over.

But for the first time in years,

I had hope.

6:06. The Return to Guy's Hospital

The following week, Dad and I found ourselves back on the train to London for another appointment at Guy's Hospital. This time, I had ensured that the appointment was scheduled after 11 a.m. to take advantage of the off-peak train fare.

Every penny mattered now, and cutting costs wherever possible was essential.

Leaving the house provided a much-needed change of scenery. Despite my skin being at its worst, swollen, covered in yellow scabs it felt good to be out.

The stares were inevitable.

People glanced, then quickly looked away.

Some probably wondered if I was contagious.

The urge to scratch was relentless, but I suppressed it, not wanting to draw more attention.

Before leaving, I spent considerable time in the bathroom, attempting to remove the dry, flaky skin from my face. This often led to painful splits, but I felt compelled to make myself as presentable as possible.

The metallic odour from the edema still clung to me.

No amount of aftershave could mask it.

My hands, riddled with splits, sometimes between 20 to 60 at a time, were useless for handling money.

I had become too embarrassed to extend my hands to receive change. Instead, I would tell cashiers to keep it, even though I couldn't afford such generosity.

We grabbed our usual coffees at the station and settled into our seats. The rhythmic clatter of the train wheels was oddly soothing as we journeyed through the English countryside.

The route from Canterbury to London offered a blend of urban and rural vistas, rolling hills, charming villages, and historical landmarks like Rochester Castle and Cathedral. Seeing these ancient structures standing tall amidst modern life always struck a chord with me.

Dad and I chatted about mundane topics,

Family gossip.

The latest news.

These conversations, though trivial, were precious. They provided a sense of normalcy in an otherwise chaotic time.

Sharing a laugh with Dad, even if brief, felt like a balm to my weary soul.

6:07. Navigating London - The Overwhelming Cityscape

Arriving at St Pancras International, the station was buzzing with activity.

The symphony of rolling suitcases.

Distant announcements echoing overhead.

The murmur of conversations in countless languages.

Navigating through the crowd, we made our way to the Underground and boarded the Northern Line to London Bridge.

The Tube experience was its usual chaotic self.

The whoosh of arriving trains.

The occasional gust of warm air from the tunnels.
The press of bodies, too close for comfort.
Every bump, every jostle sent pain rippling through my
hypersensitive skin.
Exiting at London Bridge, we were greeted by The Shard,
its towering glass facade reflecting the city's relentless
motion. A short walk later, we reached Guy's Hospital.

6.08. Back in the Dermatology Waiting Room

One thing I appreciated about Guy's was their efficiency,
I rarely had to wait long.
Yet, as I sat in the waiting room, I observed others
scratching, shifting uncomfortably.
I had the urge to share my experiences with Topical
Steroid Withdrawal (TSW).
I wanted to tell them they weren't alone.
But looking as I did, raw, swollen, flaking, who would
take me seriously?
One day, I told myself, my journey would serve as proof.
For now, I just sat quietly, waiting for my name to be
called.
The nurse called my name, and I followed her into the
consultation room. The doctor greeted me with a
professional nod before reviewing my blood test results.
Results:
Mostly normal.
Slightly elevated creatinine levels.
They weren't overly concerned but would continue

monitoring it.

Then came the big proposal.

"We want to start you on Metoject, a 25 mg injection of Methotrexate."

6:09. Metoject - A Risky but Tempting Offer

Methotrexate is an immunosuppressant commonly used to treat rheumatoid arthritis and psoriasis.

How it works:

Decreases inflammation.

Slows the overactive immune response.

But it wasn't without risk.

Nausea.

Fatigue.

Mouth sores.

Liver damage.

Increased risk of infections.

Alongside this, they also suggested a 5-day inpatient stay in their day centre for intensive steroid-free treatment.

I agreed to the inpatient treatment but requested time to research Metoject further.

Back home, I delved into the literature.

I was hesitant to start an immunosuppressant.

But I was also desperate.

This wasn't a steroid. And at this point, I had little to lose.

I recalled Dr. Rapaport mentioning that some of his patients had used Ciclosporin during Topical Steroid Withdrawal (TSW) and were later weaned off it.

Ciclosporin hadn't worked for me.

But maybe Methotrexate would.

Two days later, Guy's Hospital called.

They had a spot available after the weekend.

They asked if I had made a decision about Metoject.

I had.

"I'll do it."

- I would begin Methotrexate.

- I would go inpatient for treatment.

- I would see if this was the turning point I had been waiting for.

This was it.

The next phase of my journey had begun.

6:10. Inpatient Treatment at Guy's Hospital

Monday morning arrived, marking the start of my inpatient treatment at Guy's Hospital. After three long months of being housebound, trapped inside with nothing but pain and frustration, the idea of finally receiving proper medical attention should have been a relief.

But instead, I felt uneasy.

My skin was at an all-time low.

Red, raw, and unbearably itchy.

Every movement sent waves of discomfort through my body.

I was used to this by now, but venturing out alone, in this state, was daunting.

Still, I told myself that at least this would give my family a much-needed break from me. They had suffered alongside me for months, enduring my sleepless nights, my constant complaints, the sheer weight of my suffering.

Maybe my absence, even for a short while, would allow them to breathe again.

6:11. The Journey to London - A Test of Endurance

I got into my car and set off for my parents' house, scratching all the way. No matter how hard I tried to resist, the itching was impossible to ignore.

By the time I arrived, my skin felt like it was on fire.

I parked up, said a quick goodbye, and made my way to the train station.

The journey to London was as uncomfortable as ever.

The heat in the train carriage made my skin feel tight and inflamed.

Passengers stared, some out of curiosity, others with poorly concealed concern.

I pulled my sleeves down, kept my head low, and tried to focus on just getting through it.

Arriving at Guy's Hospital, I checked in at my usual place. I had been here a couple of times before, but this time felt different.

This wasn't just an appointment.

This time, they were keeping me.

A nurse led me to my room, a small space with a private bathroom.

Not a traditional hospital ward.

Functional, clinical, and most importantly, quiet.

For now, all I could do was settle in and brace myself for whatever was to come.

6:12. The Intensive Treatment Plan

As soon as I settled in, I barely had a moment to process my surroundings before the doctors and dermatology team arrived.

They wasted no time in outlining the intensive therapy plan they had designed for me.

Multiple treatments.

Each targeting different aspects of my condition.

A last-ditch effort to stabilise my skin.

I listened carefully. I had heard the phrase "intensive therapy" before.

Steroids. Immunosuppressants. Moisturisers. Oral medications.

None of them had worked long-term.

Why should this be any different?

But at this point, I had little choice.

My skin was deteriorating every day.

I needed to try something.

I was out of options.

The treatment's Guy's was giving me:

1. 50/50 White Soft Paraffin & Liquid Paraffin.
What is it?
A thick emollient, 50% white soft paraffin, 50% liquid paraffin.
Why was I being given this?
My skin couldn't retain moisture. This would act as a shield.
It would reduce itchiness by keeping my skin soft and supple.
It would protect open wounds from dust, bacteria, and irritants.
How it would be applied:
Smeared over my entire body at regular intervals.
Used in combination with wet wrap therapy.
Downside:

Extremely greasy, left everything I touched covered in oil.
Highly flammable, a serious fire hazard if absorbed into clothing or bedsheets.
At this point, I didn't care. If it helped, I'd deal with the mess.

2. Hydromol Ointment
What is it?
A thicker, hydrating emollient containing urea to soften skin and reduce scaling.
My skin was shedding alarmingly, this would help.

It would relieve tightness and burning.
Used under wet wraps for deeper penetration.
Downside:

Didn't allow skin to breathe, felt suffocating.

3. Wet Wrap Therapy
What is it?

A treatment for severe eczema, using damp bandages soaked in emollients to force hydration deep into the skin.

Why was I being given this?

- My skin was in extreme distress.
- Would reduce inflammation, redness, swelling, and burning.
- Acted as a barrier, stopping me from scratching in my sleep.

Downside:

- Uncomfortable, damp fabric clinging to raw skin.
- Time-consuming, required multiple applications daily.
- Made me cold, wrapped in damp bandages for hours.

4. Antiseptic Creams for Infection Prevention
What is it?

Medicated antibacterial and antifungal creams for open wounds.

My skin was a breeding ground for bacteria.
Even a small infection could spiral out of control.

How it would be applied:

Only on areas that looked infected or inflamed.

5. Dermol 500 - Antimicrobial Wash
What is it?
A soap substitute with antimicrobial properties.
Regular soap was too harsh.
Would allow me to wash without stripping my skin further.
How it would be used:
Instead of soap in the shower.
Could also be used as a leave-in moisturiser.

6. Metoject (Methotrexate) - The Biggest Decision Yet
I had never given myself an injection before now, I had to learn how to inject myself every week.
Methotrexate was an immunosuppressant.
Designed to calm my overactive immune system.
Aimed to reduce inflammation beyond the surface.

I nodded as the doctor explained it, but all I could think was:
How the hell am I going to do this?
For now, I had no choice but to trust the process.

6:13. The First Shower in Months - A Necessary Torture

Before starting wet wrap therapy, I had to be clean.
I hadn't showered in months.
Epsom salt baths had been my only relief.
The thought of standing under a showerhead terrified me.
The moment the first drop hit my skin, I jumped back in pain.
It was like scalding liquid pouring over raw wounds.
My nerve endings were on fire.
I can't do this.
But I had no choice.
Slowly, I forced myself under the water.
Reduced the pressure to a trickle.
Adjusted the temperature to lukewarm.
Every second was agony.
After surviving the shower, I noticed something waiting for me,
A cup of tea.
A couple of plain biscuits.
Such a simple thing. But in that moment?
It felt like a lifeline.
For the first time in days, I allowed myself to breathe.

My skin was like elephant skin and so fragile.

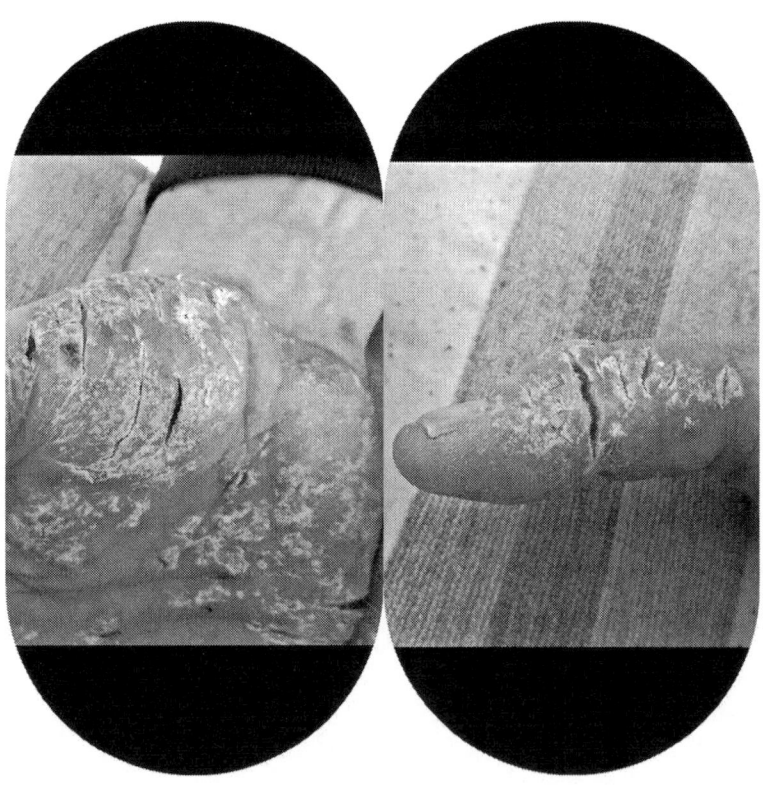

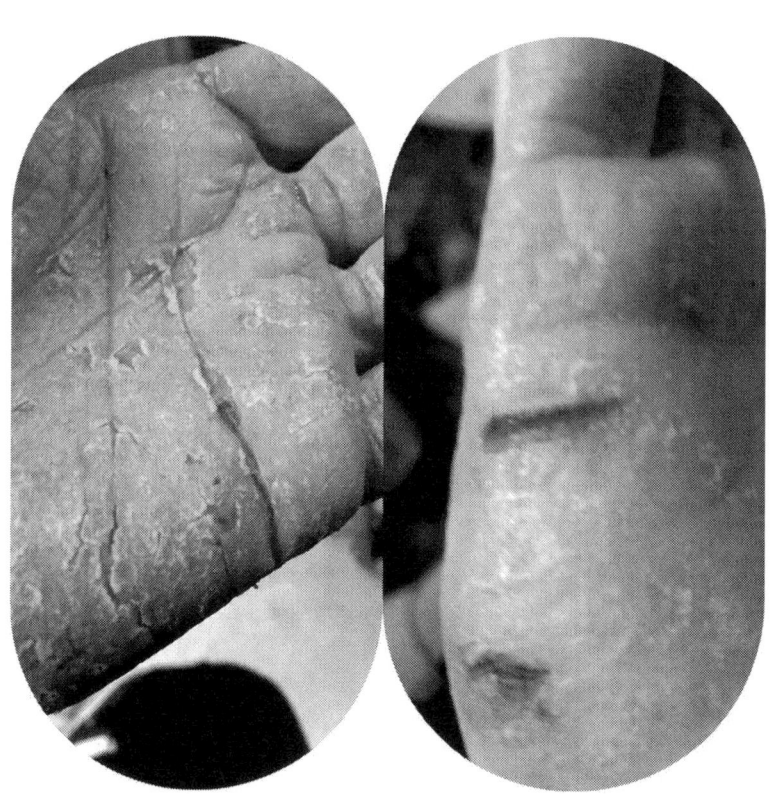

6:14. The Wet Wrap Process Begins

The nurse returned and explained that we would be
starting wet wrap therapy, a treatment I had read about
but had never actually experienced.

She asked me to sit on the hospital bed while she
prepared the 50/50 white soft paraffin and liquid paraffin
cream. The large plastic tub sat on the table beside us, the
lid already off, revealing the thick, greasy ointment inside.

Step 1: Applying the Emollient.

She scooped a generous amount into her hands, warming
it slightly between her palms before gently applying it to
my skin.

The first contact was jarring.

Not because it was painful, but because it was soothing.

I wasn't used to soothing feelings anymore. It had been
so long since I had felt any kind of relief that even the
cool glide of the ointment over my inflamed, burning
skin felt almost surreal.

- She started with my arms, rubbing the 50/50
  mixture generously over my forearms, wrists, and
  hands.

- Then, my legs, smoothing the cream over my
  shins, knees, and calves, carefully avoiding the
  deep cracks on my feet.

- Next, my chest and back, the coolness spreading
  across my itchy, red skin in slow, controlled
  strokes.

- Finally, my neck and any remaining exposed areas
  were covered.

The cream sat heavily on my skin, forming a thick, protective barrier, locking in moisture and preventing further water loss.

Step 2: The First Layer - Wet Bandages
Once my skin was fully coated, she moved on to the first layer of the wet wraps.
What is it?
Wet wrap therapy involves two layers of dressings, the first layer is damp to help soothe and rehydrate the skin, while the second layer is dry to lock everything in place.

- She took a set of special, soft cotton wraps and soaked them in warm water.
- She wrung them out so they weren't dripping, but were still moist enough to provide the cooling, hydrating effect.
- Piece by piece, she carefully wrapped them around my arms and legs, smoothing them down so they sat snugly against my skin, but weren't too tight.

The dampness of the bandages immediately felt soothing, like a cool compress against the constant burning sensation that had plagued me for so long.
The wet layer worked in two major ways:

- Helped the emollients absorb deeper into my skin, providing maximum hydration.
- Physically stopped me from scratching, acting as a barrier against my instinct to tear at my skin.

Step 3: The Second Layer - Dry Bandages
Once the wet layer was secured, she began applying the second set of bandages, the dry layer.

- These were thicker, cotton wraps designed to hold the moisture in place and regulate temperature.
- She wrapped them over the wet layers, carefully securing them around my arms, legs, and torso.
- Each wrap was smoothed down, ensuring they stayed in place without shifting as I moved.
- Finally, she tucked in the edges neatly to prevent friction against my skin.
  The second layer helped by:
- Preventing the wet wraps from drying out too quickly.
- Keeping warmth in, so I wouldn't feel cold from the damp wraps.
- Providing extra protection against scratching or irritation from clothing.
  Once everything was secured, I was fully wrapped.
  My entire body was encased in layers of moisture and protection.

How Long Were the Wraps Left On?
For severe cases like mine, wet wraps were typically left on for 2 to 6 hours during the day.
Some patients even slept in them overnight, depending on individual tolerance.

Since it was my first time, they would start with shorter sessions and see how my skin responded.

Final Steps & Immediate Effects
Once everything was in place, she asked how I was feeling.
For the first time in months, I felt cool relief.
The itching hadn't completely vanished, but it was muted.
The burning had eased.
My skin had been so dehydrated for so long, could feel the moisture sinking in.
She checked to make sure everything was comfortable, then smiled.
"You're doing well. We'll check back in a couple of hours."
As she left the room, I leaned back against the bed, staring at the ceiling.
For the first time in a long time, I didn't feel like I was burning alive.
For now, that was enough.

6:15. The Afternoon Routine

Two hours later, the nurse returned to remove the dressings.
What had started as soothing relief had become irritating.
At first, the cool moisture of the wraps had calmed the burning and itching.
But as time passed, things started to shift:

Drying and Tightness - The wet layer began to dry out, making my skin feel constricted.

Increased Sensitivity - My hypersensitive skin reacted to even the slightest fabric shift.

Rebound Itching - When the moisture wore off, my deep, relentless itching returned.

Lack of Movement - Being wrapped in layers for ages made me restless and hot.

The relief had been temporary, but it had been real.

When the nurse began peeling off the dressings, I felt relieved but also uneasy.

Without the wraps, I was once again fully exposed to the elements.

Post-Wrap Care - Sealing in Moisture

As she removed the last layer, my skin felt slightly softer, but it was still fragile, inflamed, and unbearably itchy.

She applied another thick layer of 50/50 ointment, rubbing it gently over my arms, legs, and torso.

This would seal in as much moisture as possible before leaving me to rest.

6:16. A Small Escape - Lunch at the Canteen

The hospital provided me with a £5 food voucher each day, which covered a basic meal. It wasn't much, but at least it was something.

I made my way to the canteen, which was just a short walk from the ward. The route was simple, but every step felt uncomfortable, my skin raw and tight, the fresh ointment making my clothes stick to me.

180

Ryan Thomson
The Eczema Deception

The canteen itself was a standard NHS hospital cafeteria, nothing fancy, just:
- Rows of trays
- Pre-packaged sandwiches
- A few hot meal options
- A drinks station

Most people around me were:
- Staff members in scrubs
- Patients with hospital wristbands
- Visitors grabbing a quick bite

I felt out of place. Not because I didn't belong, but because I was hyper-aware of how I looked.

I could feel the occasional glance in my direction.

I could see the subtle hesitations from people sitting near me.

My red, flaky, swollen skin made me look like a burn victim.

I ignored it, grabbed a simple meal, and found a quiet corner.

Eating felt strange.

My body was so consumed by discomfort that hunger barely registered anymore.

But I forced myself to finish my food, knowing I needed the energy to endure the rest of the day.

After lunch, I returned to the ward for another round of emollient application.

That was my life now.

Laying in a hospital bed.

Covered in thick layers of cream.

Trying not to scratch myself raw.

6:17. Gassiot House - My Temporary Home

Since this was a day surgery unit, they didn't have
overnight hospital wards, which meant they provided
alternative accommodation for patients needing to stay in
London.
I was given a room at Gassiot House, which was located
right outside St. Thomas' Hospital, at the end of
Westminster Bridge.
Gassiot House (sometimes called Gassiot Lodge) is a
hospital accommodation building used for:
Patients who need daily outpatient treatments but don't
live close enough to commute.
Families of patients in critical care or long-term hospital
stays.
NHS staff needing temporary housing when working
long shifts or relocating.
It wasn't a hotel, and it definitely wasn't luxury.
Functional
Basic.
Slightly outdated.
But it served its purpose.
When I arrived at Gassiot House, I wasn't expecting
much, and I was right.
A small, plain room with:

A single bed

A chair.

A small bedside table.

A wardrobe.

No en-suite bathroom, just a shared one down the hall.

A communal kitchen with:

A microwave.

A kettle.

A fridge to store food.

It was a far cry from comfort.

But the location was incredible, right in the heart of London, overlooking the River Thames, with,

Westminster Bridge

Big Ben

The Houses of Parliament

Just a short walk away.

6:18. A Long, Sleepless Night at Gassiot House

After finishing my last round of emollient applications, I made my way outside to catch the free minibus that ran between:

Guy's Hospital - St. Thomas' Hospital

The bus ran every 15 minutes

It was mainly for patients, staff, and long-term treatment cases.

As I boarded the bus, I sank into the seat, feeling exhausted yet restless, a familiar state by now.

The ride was short, winding through the busy London streets.

The city was alive, people, traffic, movement.
It felt surreal.
For most, London was a place of:

Work
Tourism
Excitement
For me?
It was just another stop in my battle to reclaim my skin.
I got off at St. Thomas' Hospital, the towering building
standing against the night sky, its windows glowing under
the city lights.

Before heading to Gassiot House, I stopped at the
hospital shop to grab some snacks, something light to get
me through the night.

Back in my small, plain room, I set my things down, took
a deep breath, and dialed home.
Hearing my family's voices on the other end of the line
was both comforting and painful.
I asked how the kids were, how their day had gone, and
tried to sound as normal as possible, even though I felt
anything but.
My wife updated me on their routines, school, and little
moments from the day, things that I should have been
home to experience myself.
The guilt crept in again.
Even though I knew I was here for the right reasons, it
was hard to shake the feeling that:

I was letting them down.

I was missing out on their lives.

I was trapped in my own personal nightmare.
I reassured them that I was okay, even though I wasn't. I had to be strong for them.
After the call, I put my phone down, stared at the ceiling for a moment, and sighed heavily.
I was overcome with emotions, I felt alone, let down and desperate, I lay there in tears feeling extremely sorry for myself, why me?

A Night That Felt Like an Eternity
I had barely been sleeping at home, so I had no illusions that I'd sleep any better here.
But this bed was worse, thin mattress, stiff and unyielding, the kind of bed that makes you count every minute you lie on it.
I adjusted the pillows, shifted positions, but nothing helped.
The itch came in waves, unrelenting, growing worse with every passing hour.
I scratched my arms, feeling the rough, broken skin beneath my fingertips.
I scratched my legs, my feet, and my back, until I felt the wetness of new wounds opening up again.
I tried to stop, but it was impossible.
Every time I thought I had worn myself out enough to drift off, another surge of itching would hit, snapping me back to full awareness.
I glanced at the clock.

1:45 AM.

3:30 AM.

4:55 AM.

It was endless.

Late in to Month 4, the sleep deprivation had improved.

But this?

This was still Month 3.

I was still in the worst of it.

Still waking up raw and bleeding every morning.

The hours dragged on, the night feeling never-ending, as I lay there.

Covered in moisturisers and bandages.

My skin both soothed and tormented at the same time.

The only thought keeping me going was that Morning will come soon.

If I could just get through the night,

I could take the minibus back to Guy's.

Get some breakfast.

And get out of this room.

6:19. Learning To Inject Metoject

Morning finally arrived.

Another sleepless, itchy night behind me.

I wasted no time getting up.

Washed my face.

Brushed my teeth.

Gathered my things.

The First Goal of the Day? Breakfast.

Take the minibus back to Guy's Hospital.

Get some breakfast.

The bus ride was short, but the relief of being back in motion, out of that small room, and heading toward a routine helped shake off the exhaustion from the night before.

Breakfast felt more like a proper meal compared to what was offered for lunch.

Freshly cooked eggs, sausages, beans, toast, simple but hearty.

The smell of coffee and hot food filled the canteen, making it a surprisingly comforting place despite being in a hospital.

I used my £5 food voucher, picked out something filling, and sat down in a quiet spot to eat.

For the first time in hours, I felt somewhat normal.

After finishing up, I headed back to my room, took another shower, carefully adjusting the temperature and water pressure before stepping in.

My skin still stung under the water, but it was necessary.

Cleaned up and ready for the day, I waited for the doctor's visit.

6:20. The Doctor's Visit - Time for Metoject

The doctor arrived, checked in on me, and asked how I was feeling.

I told him the truth.

The itching was still relentless.

The sleepless nights weren't improving yet.

The wet wraps had helped, but only temporarily.
After a quick chat, I was sent for blood tests and vital checks.
Blood pressure taken.
Heart rate monitored.
Routine blood work to make sure everything was stable before starting the Metoject.
Then came the Metoject injection.
The nurse came in carrying the injection pen, explaining how I would need to administer it myself going forward.
The process was similar to an EpiPen.
A preloaded injection that delivers the medication just beneath the skin.

Step-by-Step Process of Taking the Metoject Injection

1, Choose the Injection Site.

Either side of my stomach (at least two inches away from my belly button).
The tops of my thighs.
They advised against using the arms, not enough fatty tissue for proper absorption.

2, Clean the Injection Site

Use an alcohol swab to clean the area before injecting.

3, Prepare the Pen

The Metoject comes preloaded, just remove the cap and it's ready.

4, Position the Injection Pen.
Hold the pen at a 90-degree angle against the skin.
Press it firmly but not forcefully.

5, Press the Button to Inject

Once positioned, press the activation button.
The needle shoots out automatically, delivering the dose
in seconds.

6, Hold for 10 Seconds

Keep the injector pressed against the skin for 10 seconds
before removing it.

7, Dispose of the Pen Safely

The used pen goes into a sharps container, no recapping,
no reusing.

Why Switch Injection Sites?
The nurse emphasised the importance of rotating the
injection sites each week.
Prevents skin irritation.
Ensures better absorption.
Avoids fat loss (lipoatrophy).
Reduces pain & sensitivity.
The plan was simple.
One week on the left side of my stomach.
The next week on the right.

Then alternate to my thighs.

The thought of sticking a needle into myself every week?

Not something I was looking forward to.

But I had no choice.

If this was part of my journey to recovery, I had to push through it.

Processing It All

Once the injection was done, the nurse gave me some final reminders:

Expect some fatigue.

Watch for side effects like nausea or dizziness.

Take it at the same time each week.

Always dispose of used pens properly.

I sat there for a moment, taking it all in.

Another treatment. Another routine.

Would this finally be the thing that worked?

Would this turn things around?

Or was I just adding another medication to the long list of failed attempts?

I didn't know.

All I could do was stick to the plan,

and hope for the best.

6:21. A Small Escape to Borough Market

The rest of the second morning at Guy's Hospital followed the same routine,

Emollients applied.

Thick layers of ointment smoothed over my burning

skin.

Lying on the bed, trying to relax in the discomfort.

At this point, "relaxing" wasn't really possible, I could only shift between different states of discomfort, never truly finding relief.

The itch never stopped.

The burning never faded completely.

The greasy layers of moisturisers made every movement feel slow and sticky.

It was exhausting.

Physically.

Mentally.

Emotionally.

By lunchtime, I needed to get out of that room, even for just a short while.

I decided to skip the hospital canteen this time and take a short walk to Borough Market instead.

I wasn't looking forward to the effort, but I needed:

Fresh air.

A change of scenery.

A taste of something that didn't come from a hospital tray.

So I got dressed, pulling on my clothes over the thick layer of grease covering my body, knowing full well I was probably leaving:

A snail trail of ointment.

A flake trail of dead skin.

A reminder of my condition with every step I took.

I didn't care. I just needed to feel normal, if only for half an hour.

Borough Market was only a few minutes away, but every

step felt heavier than usual.

My skin felt suffocated under the layers of moisturisers.

My clothes stuck to me, every movement tugging against the greasy barrier.

The wind hit my exposed hands and face, making them feel even drier than before.

The sun felt too bright, making the redness of my skin stand out even more.

But despite all that, I was glad to be outside.

The world still felt normal, and for a brief moment, that was nice.

But at the same time, it was frustrating,

watching everyone else go about their day.

Feeling like I was the only person in the world trapped in this condition.

No one else looked like they were suffering.

No one else looked like they wanted to claw their skin off every second of the day.

They were laughing, eating, walking freely,

while I was dragging my raw, swollen, greasy body through the crowd, trying not to let the irritation and exhaustion consume me.

Borough Market was one of my favourite places in London.

It had that bustling energy,

A mix of tourists and locals.

Food vendors shouting out their specials.

The constant smell of fresh food being cooked right in front of you.

I had one stall in mind, the one that did proper breakfast rolls but also had other amazing fillings.

I made my way over, scanning the menu even though I

already knew exactly what I wanted.

Lamb, mint jelly, and rocket, my absolute favourite.

It was hot, fresh, packed with flavour, the kind of food that felt like a treat, even when I barely had an appetite anymore.

I sat down for a few minutes, sipping on a Diet Coke, watching the world carry on around me.

I wasn't healed.

I wasn't better.

But for half an hour, I wasn't just a hospital patient covered in ointment, waiting for another round of treatment.

I was just a person having lunch in London.

And I needed that.

After finishing my food, I took one last deep breath of fresh air, stood up, and started the short walk back to the hospital.

The moment I stepped inside, the hospital smell hit me again,

that clinical, sterile scent that reminded me exactly why I was here.

My next wet wrap session was waiting for me.

Back to the routine.

Back to lying in bed, trying not to scratch.

Back to the fight.

6:22. A Conversation That Needed to Happen

I made my way back to my hospital room, feeling the weight of exhaustion settling back onto me.

The brief escape to Borough Market had been a mental break, but as soon as I walked through the hospital doors,

I was right back in the cycle.

Back to the Wet Wraps.

The nurse came in shortly after, the familiar Swedish woman who had been looking after me since I arrived.

She didn't say much, she just got to work.

Smothering me in emollients once again.

Thick layers of 50/50 white soft paraffin and liquid paraffin.

Sealing my dry, cracked, and burning skin under its suffocating yet necessary embrace.

Then came the wet wraps, the process I was still trying to get used to.

She wrapped my limbs carefully, making sure the damp layer was snug but not too tight.

Then the dry layer was added on top, locking in the moisture and preventing the intense evaporation that could make the skin even drier.

For the first ten minutes, it was:

Cooling.
Calming.
A relief.
But as the hour passed, the feeling shifted.

194

The itching crept in.

The tightness of the wraps started to irritate me.

The restlessness returned.

Then, the door opened.

A man walked in, mid-forties, dressed in smart-casual clothes, with an expression that was both professional and laid-back.

He introduced himself as Mark, the dermatology ward psychiatrist.

I hadn't expected this.

I hadn't asked to see anyone, but as soon as he sat down, I realised how much I needed this conversation.

For the next hour, I let everything out.

I told him everything.

The financial toll this had taken.

How work was falling apart.

The stress at home.

The strain on my marriage.

The complete and utter exhaustion I felt every single day.

I hadn't really spoken about this with anyone properly before.

Doctors? Most had barely even acknowledged how much this was destroying my life outside of the physical symptoms.

Friends? They tried to be supportive, but they couldn't truly understand.

My wife? She knew how bad things were, but we were both too deep in it to even process it properly.

But Mark understood.

He listened.

He didn't try to sugar-coat anything.

He treated me like a person, not just a patient.

For the first time in a long time, I felt a tiny bit lighter, just from talking to someone who truly got it.

I still felt drained.

I still felt like my life was in free fall.

But I wasn't alone in it anymore.

And for now, that was enough.

6:23. A Small Escape - Walking to Tesco Extra

When the day was over I got the mini bus back to Gassiot House, I didn't want to sit in the depressing room so I rolled myself a joint, tucked it away, and walked down to Tesco Extra to grab something to eat. Nothing fancy, just a meal deal, something quick and familiar.

I wasn't even that hungry, but I knew I had to eat.

Food had become more of a task than a pleasure lately, something I had to force myself to do rather than something I actually enjoyed.

I walked through the bright, artificial lights of the Tesco aisles, picked out a sandwich, a snack, and a bottle of Diet Coke, paid, and headed out into the night.

I found a quiet spot by the river, away from the crowds, where I could sit in peace.

The Thames stretched out in front of me, the city lights reflecting off its surface, the sound of water lapping

against the banks mixed with the muffled hum of
London in the background.
For a moment, it felt like I was just another person in the
city,
Rather than a hospital patient covered in ointment and
bandages.
I ate my sandwich in silence, taking small bites, barely
tasting it.
Then, I lit up the joint.
As I smoked, I let my mind wander.
How long is this going to take?

Will I ever fully recover?

How much more of this can I handle?
I didn't have answers to any of it.
And that was the hardest part.
The uncertainty.
The not knowing when, or if, this would ever truly end.
Watching life carry on around me, normal people, doing
normal things,
While I was stuck in this nightmare, it was frustrating.
I wasn't jealous of them, not really.

I just wanted to feel like them again.
To not have to think about my skin every waking second.
To not feel like a prisoner inside my own body.
After a while, I put my headphones in, finished the last
few drags, and started walking back to Gassiot House.
I didn't feel amazing.

But I felt a little bit lighter.

Just enough.

Enough to get back to my room, lay down, and accept that this was home for the next while.

Enough to drift off for an hour, which, compared to the night before, was progress.

And as I lay there, half-awake, half-asleep, I realised something:

Maybe this won't last forever.

Maybe, eventually, I'll find my way back to normal.

Maybe, for now, I just need to keep going.

6:24. A Walk Through London & A Close Call

By Day 3, I noticed something small, but significant.

The swelling in my feet had gone down slightly.

Not a lot, but enough that they didn't feel as painfully tight as the day before.

It wasn't much, but it was the only positive change I had felt in months, so I took it.

Maybe I'd hit the peak of the flare?

Maybe things were starting to turn around?

It was just a tiny bit of hope, but after everything I'd been through, I clung onto it like my life depended on it.

The Same Hospital Routine

Day 3 at the hospital was much like the others, the same intensive treatments, the same routine.

Dermol 500 shower to cleanse the skin without stripping

away what little barrier I had left.

Emollients applied thickly, 50/50 white soft paraffin and liquid paraffin, layered on like a second skin.

Wet wraps covering my arms and legs, cooling at first, then irritating as time passed.

More emollients, more monitoring, more of the same.

The days in the hospital felt slow, the hours dragging by as I lay there, trying not to scratch, and feeling like I was in some kind of never-ending loop.

By the evening, I had had enough.

I needed to get out of this room.

I needed to move.

It was a warm evening, and my feet, while still swollen, felt just about good enough to walk on.

So I rolled a couple of joints, put them in my pocket, and set off on a walk.

I walked past Parliament Square, the evening lights glowing softly against the historic buildings.

The air was warm, the city still alive but not as chaotic as during the day.

For the first time in months, I felt a little bit normal.

I was outside, walking through London, instead of lying in a hospital bed, waiting for time to pass.

I carried on, heading towards Nelson's Column, then down The Mall.

By the time I reached St. James's Park, I was feeling tired, but in a good way.

I found a quiet bench, one with a clear view of Buckingham Palace in the distance.

The park was calm, the sound of gentle chatter and rustling trees filling the evening air.

I sat down, cracked open a can of Monster, took a deep breath, and lit a joint.

For the first time in a long time, I felt a little bit of peace.

The walking had felt better, not great, but better.

Maybe there really was a sign of hope.

Maybe I was finally turning a corner.

I exhaled, watching the smoke disappear into the night.

And then I felt it.

A tap on my shoulder.

I turned around, and there they were,

Two armed police officers, standing over me, rifles slung across their chests.

"Fuck".

"First time I venture out in months, and now I'm about to get arrested".

I could tell exactly why they were here, they must have been patrolling the park, caught a whiff of the weed, and decided to check it out.

I didn't even try to hide it, there was no point.

The joint was right there in my hand.

I took a breath, apologised straight away, and then explained myself.

"Look, I know I shouldn't be smoking here, but I'm a patient at Guy's Hospital, This is literally the only thing that gives me relief from the pain."

They didn't immediately react, just looked me over.

Then, one of them motioned to my face and hands.

I knew what he was seeing.

So I pulled out my phone, turned on the torch, and held it up so they could get a proper look.

My raw, swollen, flaking skin.
My cracked fingers, covered in tiny splits.
The deep redness that hadn't faded for months.
They took a second, looked at each other,
And then one of them spoke.
"Why don't you head over there instead?"
He pointed to a tree in the distance, away from the main path.
And that was it.
No arrest.
No lecture.
No confiscation.
Just a quiet understanding.
They turned and walked away, leaving me to finish my joint in peace.

6:25. A Needed Break & The Journey Home

The rest of my stay at Guy's Hospital was pretty uneventful.
Each day followed the same pattern,
Morning checks - Blood work, vitals, making sure the Metoject wasn't causing any immediate issues.
Intensive treatments- and just lying there, waiting.
Evenings at Gassiot House - Trying to find a way to pass the time, attempting to sleep through the relentless itch.
Though not much changed, I could see small

improvements.

The swelling in my feet was very slowly easing.

The tightness in my skin didn't feel quite as suffocating.

It wasn't much, but I'd take anything.

One night, I felt brave enough to go a little further.

I needed a change of scenery.

So I took a walk down to Chinatown, craving something different from hospital food.

It was a cheap, all-you-can-eat buffet, one of those places where the food had been sitting out for a while, but at that moment, I didn't care.

I wasn't particularly hungry, my appetite was still nowhere near normal, but I thought:

Screw it, I'll try.

I probably didn't eat my money's worth, just a small plate here and there, but the act of sitting in a restaurant again, being around normal life, felt like a step in the right direction.

After dinner, I walked through Leicester Square, passing all the bright lights, the street performers, and the crowds of tourists.

It was busy, but I felt detached from it all, watching life carry on as normal while I was still stuck in my own battle.

Then I saw it,

Legends was still showing at one of the cinemas.

It was the film about the Kray twins, with Tom Hardy playing both brothers.

I had wanted to see it for a while, but was in no condition

too.

Now, I had time, and if the itching got too bad, I could just leave.

So I went inside, bought a ticket, and found my seat.
To my relief, there was only one other person in the entire cinema.
No one around to stare at my skin.
No one to feel self-conscious around.
Just me, a dark room, and a film.
For the first time in a long time, I actually relaxed.
I sat through the whole thing, undisturbed, enjoying something as simple as a movie.
That night, it felt like a win.

6:26. The Journey Home - Small Progress

Then, just like that, my week at Guy's Hospital was over.
I was loaded up with supplies,
Emollients to keep my skin coated in moisture.
Dermol 500 for washing without irritation.
Metoject injections and a biohazard bin to safely dispose of the used needles.
It wasn't a cure, but it was a plan.
I made my way to the tube, dragging my suitcase full of medical supplies, ready to head home.
Looking back on that week, I realised something.
It had been a needed break.

A break from being stuck at home, isolated.

A break from feeling completely alone in this battle.

A break from the monotony of suffering in the same four walls.

My skin?

Still a mess, still far from healed, but slightly, just slightly, better.

The swelling had gone down a little more each day.

I felt like maybe, just maybe, I had turned a small corner.

For the first time in months, I felt a bit more positive.

I knew there was still a long road ahead, but for now, I had made it through another step of the journey.

"For the first time in months, I had a glimpse of hope. It wasn't much. But hope, however small, was something I could hold onto."

Chapter 7. The Long Road to Recovery

7:01. Reduced Swelling

I arrived back home from Guy's Hospital feeling a little more positive than when I left.

Not because I was better, because I wasn't.

But because, for the first time in a long time, I felt like there was a direction.

A plan.

Something other than just waking up every day to face the same unrelenting hell without knowing where it was leading.

My skin was still an absolute disaster, a big, red, burning, scabby mess.

The oozing hadn't let up much.

The itching still ran me ragged.

Every movement felt like my body was being torn apart from the inside out.

But one thing had changed, the swelling.

The unbearable tightness in my feet and ankles had eased just enough to notice.

I could feel my bones again, rather than the swollen, fluid-logged lumps they had become. Over the next couple of weeks, the improvement continued, little by little. The fluid that had made my feet look like they belonged to someone twice my size was draining away, slowly retreating.

It was small, but it was something.

And after months of nothing but deterioration, I clung to anything that even slightly resembled progress.

7:02. Coming Home to a Different Reality

Walking through the door, I was met with familiar sights, familiar smells, and the familiar hum of my home. But even though everything looked the same, I wasn't the same.

The children rushed to hug me, their little arms wrapping around me tightly. That moment, just feeling them close, feeling that love, was everything I had been craving.

Their smiles were genuine, their happiness at seeing me real.

But when I looked at my wife, I wasn't sure she felt the same.

There was no rush into my arms, no look of relief that I was back. Just a tired expression, a half-hearted smile, a glance that didn't quite meet my eyes.

I knew that look.

That was the look of exhaustion.

That was the look of someone who had been carrying too much, for too long.

And I knew, in that moment, that I wasn't walking back into a home where my absence had made hearts grow fonder.

I was walking back into a house that had become quieter, maybe even more peaceful, without my suffering echoing through the walls.

I had been gone, but my illness hadn't.

She had still been dealing with:

The extra washing, sheets covered in flakes of my dead skin.

The constant clean-ups.

The nights lying beside an empty space in the bed, but still being kept awake by the ghost of my suffering.

She had still been carrying the weight of it all, without me there to make it worse.

We weren't in a good place.

We hadn't been for a long time.

And I knew, deep down, that every additional day of my suffering was pushing her further away from me.

We weren't talking like we used to.

We weren't laughing like we used to.

We weren't us anymore.

How could we be, when all I had to offer was pain?

The man she had married, the strong, hardworking, reliable husband, had disappeared, swallowed whole by this condition that had turned me into a version of myself I no longer recognised.

And I could feel it, as I stood there in our home.

I was back, but I wasn't wanted.

Not in the way I used to be.

Not as the husband she had built a life with.

But as a burden.

A weight.

Another thing she had to endure.

And that hurt more than any physical agony I had ever felt.

But I was home.

And I had a plan.

For the first time in years, I had dermatologists who were actually listening to me.

Who respected my decision to fight this battle without steroids?

Who weren't treating me like a delusional idiot who had no idea what was best for his own body.

And for now, that was the only positive I had to hold onto.

It wasn't much.

But in this fight, where every single day felt like it took a piece of me, I had learned to take even the smallest victories and cling to them like lifelines.

7:03. Jojoba Oil

In my desperation to ease my suffering, I spent hours searching online, reading through forums, blog posts, and recovery stories.

And that's when I came across something I hadn't tried before:

Jojoba Oil.

What is Jojoba Oil?

- Jojoba oil is not actually an oil, it's a liquid wax ester, meaning it's structurally very similar to the natural sebum produced by human skin.

- Unlike most oils that just sit on top of the skin, jojoba can penetrate deep into the skin barrier, hydrating it from within.

- It's non-comedogenic, meaning it doesn't clog pores, making it one of the few oils safe to use on the face.

Why Does It Work for Topical Steroid Withdrawal (TSW)?

- Mimics Natural Skin Oils - Because its structure is so close to human sebum, the skin recognises it and absorbs it rather than rejecting it like heavier oils.

- Deep Hydration Without Suffocation - Unlike paraffin-based moisturisers, which create a greasy barrier, jojoba hydrates without suffocating the skin, allowing it to breathe.

- Anti-Inflammatory Properties - Helps calm redness, reduce burning sensations, and soothe irritation.

- Balances Skin - Instead of making the skin overly oily or overly dry, it regulates moisture levels.

How I Used It

- I started applying a few drops to my face every morning and night, gently massaging it into the driest areas.

- Unlike everything else I had tried, it didn't burn. It didn't just sit there uselessly, it actually soaked in.

- Within a few days, I could already see a difference, the flaking reduced, the tightness eased, and for the first time in months, I felt like my face wasn't getting worse.

Did it heal me overnight? No.

Did it stop the redness completely? No.

But did it feel like I was finally doing something that was actually helping my skin recover, rather than just masking the symptoms? Yes.

And that was enough to keep using it.

7:04. Needing to return Work - A Desperate Attempt

By 4.5 months into Topical Steroid Withdrawal (TSW), I had reached a breaking point.
I needed to get out of the house.
I needed to feel like a person again.
The house sale had finally gone through.
- The money from it had come in.
- I had paid Mark back, a relief in itself, knowing I wasn't carrying that debt over my head anymore.
But that equity?
That was now our only money.
And it wasn't a lot.
Not enough to keep us afloat indefinitely.
I had no choice.
I had to work.
I knew it was going to be a struggle.
I knew I was still far from functioning like a normal person.
But I couldn't just sit there, waiting for my body to heal while we drained every last penny we had.
So I made the decision.
I was going back to work.
I had no idea if I'd last a day, a week, or a month.
But I had to try.

7:05. Back to Work - A Battle Against My Own Body

I went back to work, apprehensive but determined.
Could I handle this?
Was I really ready?
Or was I just forcing something my body wasn't capable of yet?
I had finally started getting 1 to 2 hours of sleep a night.
That might not sound like much.
But after four months of only sleeping two hours every fourth day, it was a massive improvement.
I felt like I was on the edge of functioning again,
But only just.
Work had stocked up on plenty of gloves and cotton liners for me.
They were trying to help.
I was trying to push through.
But my body had other ideas.
The fissures in my hands deepened with every movement.
The skin on my ankles was so dry it felt like cracked leather, splitting open with each step.
The burning itch was relentless, made worse by the constant exposure to different materials, fabrics, and environments.
I forced myself through it.
Day after day.
Hour after hour.

211

I wasn't ready.

I knew I wasn't ready.

But I couldn't admit it to myself.

Then, after two weeks, my body gave out.
The flares got worse.
The cracks got deeper.
The exhaustion caught up with me.
I had no choice, I had to stop again.
Another month off work.
Another month back in the same place I had been before.
Maybe I had pushed too soon.
Maybe I should have waited longer.
Maybe it wouldn't have made a difference at all.
I didn't know.
All I knew was,
I wasn't done with this battle yet.

7:06. Trapped in Isolation Again

So there I was, stuck back at home again, feeling alone, defeated, and exhausted.
The walls felt like they were closing in on me.

The days stretched out like an endless loop of pain and waiting.

Every morning, I woke up to the same burning, the same itch, and the same torment.

I had pushed myself too soon.

And now, I was paying the price.

When you're suffering like this, when no one around you truly understands, you search for connection wherever you can find it.

For me, that meant Facebook support groups.

ITSAN - Topical Steroid Withdrawal Support Group

Topical Steroid Withdrawal & Red Skin Syndrome Support Group

These groups became my lifeline during those endless, isolating days.

Back in 2014, when I first joined, there were only a few thousand people in these groups.

Now? There are over 25,000 in each.

Is it finally becoming more widely known?

Or are more and more people suffering?

I didn't know.

Maybe it was both.

7:07. The Double-Edged Sword of Online Support

There was comfort in knowing I wasn't the only one going through this.

People shared their stories, struggles, and tips for coping
with the relentless suffering.
Some recommended certain emollients.
Some swore by dietary changes.
Some shared photos of their progress, proof that things
could, and did, get better.
But there was also something unsettling about these
groups.
The people who got better?
They left.
Once they had healed, it seemed they had moved on.
They didn't come back.
They didn't post updates.
They didn't share their success stories.
Maybe they wanted to forget.

Maybe they couldn't bear to relive it.

Maybe they had spent so long consumed by Topical
Steroid Withdrawal (TSW) that once they escaped, they
never wanted to look back.
And that's what made it so hard to believe in recovery.
 Because when you're stuck in the worst of it, all you see
are people who are still suffering.
Because they're the ones still searching for answers.
Still desperate for relief.
Still clinging to hope.
I kept asking myself:
Does anyone actually get better?

 Or do they just stop talking about it?
I wanted to believe that one day, I'd be one of those

people,
One of the ones who disappeared because they no longer
needed to be here.
But right now?
I was still drowning.
Still stuck in the nightmare.
Still searching for a way out.

7:08. The Never-Ending Cycle of Topical Steroid Withdrawal (TSW)

I don't want my story to sound repetitive,
But the truth is, Topical Steroid Withdrawal (TSW) itself
is repetitive.
It's the same cycle, over and over again.
You get a little better.
You get worse again.
You think you're healing.
Then another flare rips through you.
It's like being trapped in a cruel game where the rules
keep changing,
Where you never know if today will be a good day or a
complete disaster.
Every single day, you wake up in pain, discomfort, and
relentless itching.
And it feels like forever.
By the back end of month 5, I started seeing some real
progress.
Not fast progress.
Not dramatic progress.

But small, slow, almost unnoticeable improvements.

Day by day, my skin was very gradually getting better.

The redness was fading, not gone, but not as aggressive as before.

The oozing had mostly stopped, which was a huge relief.

My skin still felt tight, flaky, and unbearably itchy, but it wasn't as raw as before.

Was it the Methotrexate finally kicking in?

Or was it just time, allowing my body to repair itself?

I had no idea.

And honestly?

I didn't care.

All I knew was that I was moving in the right direction,

Even if it was at a snail's pace

The red itchy rash that took over the arms!

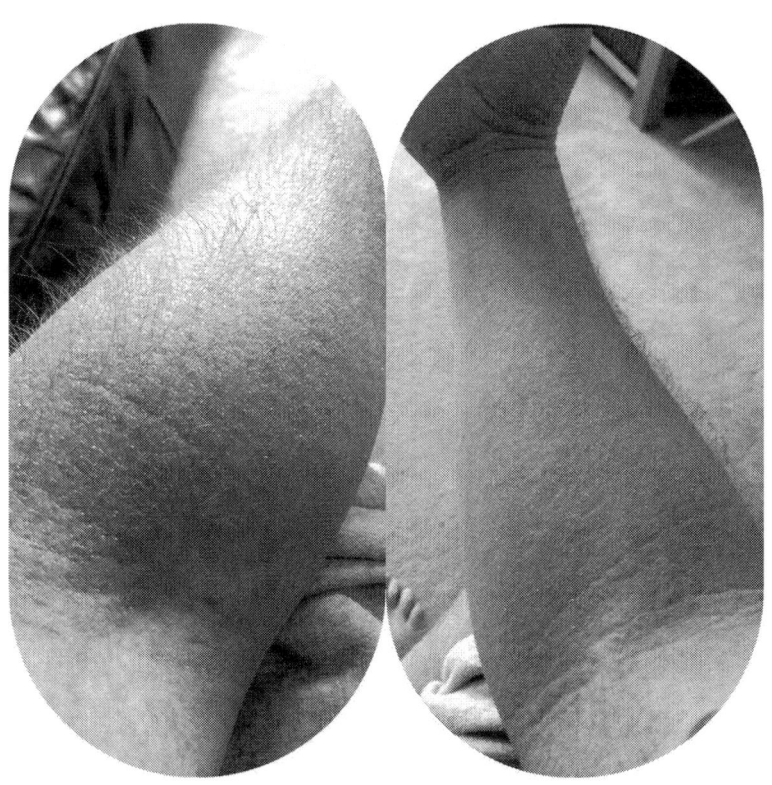

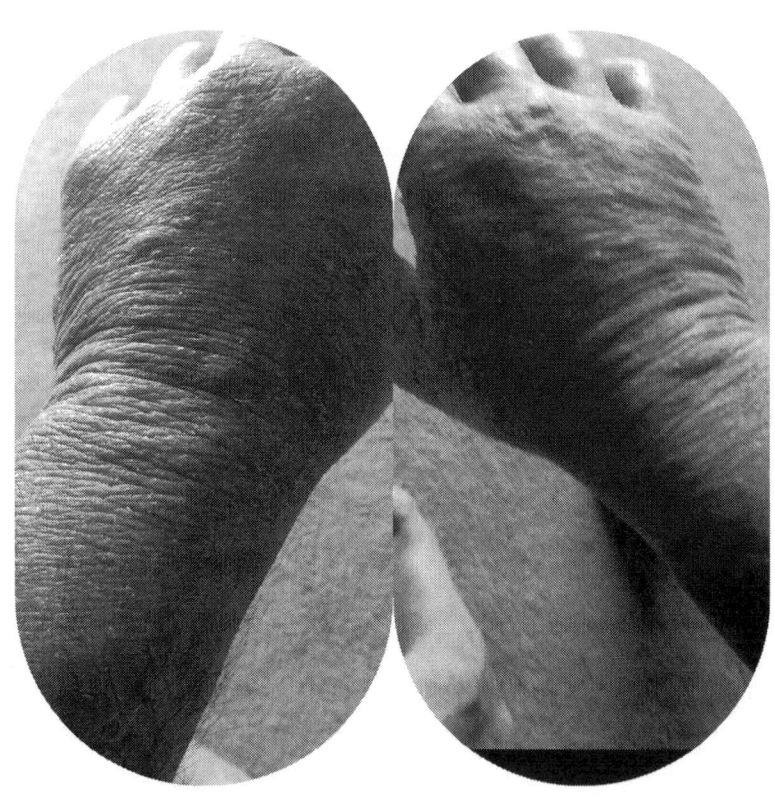

Then the rash would turn dry and flaky.

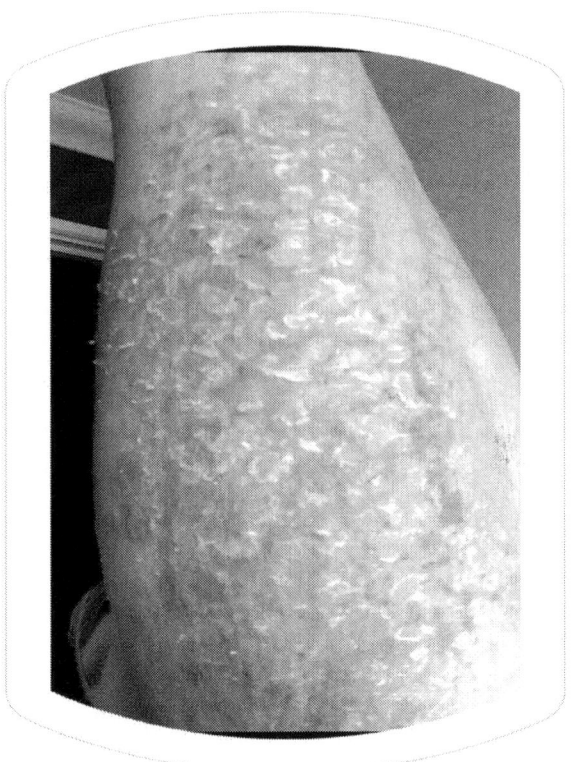

7:09. Guy's Hospital - The Bleach Bath Plan

My Guy's Hospital appointments during this time were
pretty uneventful.

There were no new treatments.

No major changes to the plan.

We just kept going with what we had already been doing.

But they did suggest one new thing,

Bleach Baths.

At first, I was skeptical.

Bathing in bleach? Seriously?

It sounded insane.

My skin was already raw and fragile, and now they
wanted me to soak it in something as harsh as bleach?

But they weren't talking about neat bleach, this was a
controlled dilution using Milton Fluid, a mild antiseptic
solution.

What Are Bleach Baths?

Bleach baths are commonly used in dermatology to help
people with:

Severe eczema

Bacterial infections

Chronic skin conditions

They work by killing bacteria on the skin's surface,
reducing the risk of infection.

They can also help calm inflammation, allowing the skin
to heal more efficiently.

How It's Done:

A small amount of Milton Fluid is added to a full bathtub
of warm water.

Soak for 10-15 minutes, no scrubbing, just letting the

diluted solution do its job.

Rinse off with fresh water and immediately apply moisturiser to prevent excessive dryness.

Did It Work?

Surprisingly, yes.

After a few weeks of doing bleach baths, my skin continued to improve.

The redness kept fading.

I had fewer open wounds.

It wasn't a miracle cure, but it definitely helped keep infections away, which, at this stage, was a huge win.

7:10. Month 6 - Time to Go Back to Work (Again)

By Month 6, I felt ready to try work again.

I knew it was risky.

I knew I wasn't fully healed.

But I had been off work for too long, and I couldn't afford to stay home forever.

This time, I was better prepared.

Armed with my 50/50 paraffin mix and Cetraben, I was determined to push through.

But the biggest questions remained:

Would I last longer than two weeks this time?

Or was I about to repeat the same mistake all over again?

I didn't know.

But I had to try.

After this, I never really had too much time off work again.

It wasn't because work had suddenly become easy, far from it.

Every single day was still a battle.

But I had reached a point where staying home wasn't an option anymore.

The job itself wasn't too physically demanding, which was a blessing.

If something was too harsh on my hands, my workmates would help out, I was lucky to have that kind of support.

My monthly hospital appointments in London were the only real time I had to take off, these trips would take up an entire day.

But despite all of this, one thing hadn't changed.

The itching was still unbearable.

7:11. The Habit Reversal Theory

At one of my monthly Guy's Hospital appointments, they suggested something new.

According to the doctors, my scratching had become a habit.

A habit?!

I couldn't believe what I was hearing.

This wasn't some mindless action.

I wasn't scratching because I was bored or stressed.

I scratched because I itched.

Simple as that.

But they insisted that I try something called Habit
Reversal Therapy (HRT).

This meant travelling to London weekly for six weeks to
work with Mark, the hospital psychiatrist.

It was yet another expense, another chunk of time off
work.

But I was willing to give it a shot, because at this stage, I
would try anything to ease the suffering.

7:12. What Is Habit Reversal Therapy?

Habit Reversal Therapy (HRT) is a psychological
treatment used for compulsive behaviours, such as:
Chronic skin picking (dermatillomania)
Hair pulling (trichotillomania)
Nail biting (onychophagia)
The idea behind it is that some repetitive behaviours
become automatic habits, things you do without thinking.
HRT helps patients recognise these behaviours and
replace them with something less harmful.

How Does It Work?
Step 1: Awareness Training
I had to actively pay attention to when and why I was
scratching.
Was it triggered by stress?
Was I doing it without realising it?

223

Did I notice a pattern?

Step 2: Competing Response Training

Instead of scratching, I had to try an alternative action whenever I felt the urge.

Clenching my fists

Pressing my hands against my thighs

Rubbing my fingers together

Step 3: Stress Management

They also suggested relaxation techniques to help manage my urges:

Deep breathing

Meditation

Even wearing gloves to act as a physical barrier

Did It Work?

No.

Not because HRT doesn't work for some people, it absolutely does.

But in my case?

The doctors were wrong.

My scratching wasn't a habit.

It wasn't compulsive.

It was because my skin was still inflamed and still itching like hell.

This wasn't a psychological issue.

This was a physical reaction to a real medical condition.

I tried their techniques.

I went to the sessions.

I did everything they asked.

But when the itch hit, Nothing could stop me from scratching.

7:13. A Slow but Steady Recovery

Even though habit reversal therapy didn't help, my skin
was improving.
It was just happening at a painfully slow pace.
Month after month, I could feel myself gradually healing.
My hands were still a mess, but the deep cracks were
healing faster.
The redness was fading, bit by bit.
I was managing work better, even though it was still
exhausting.
It wasn't a miracle breakthrough.
It wasn't like I woke up one day and felt better.
But day by day, bit by bit,
I was starting to get my life back.
I carried on with the weekly Metoject injections, week
after week, month after month.
And somewhere along the way, past the one-year mark,
something unexpected happened,
My skin started looking good.
Not perfect. Not flawless. But compared to where I had
been?
It was a massive improvement.
The first areas to heal was the places that had never been
affected before steroids?
My back, my neck, the back of the tops of my legs.

But the rest of me was still not 100%.
My face?
Still redder than usual, but not raw anymore, just a
slightly flushed complexion.

My hands and feet?
Still not great. Still damaged, still fragile.
But the aggressive, full-body flares never returned.

My elbows and forearms?
Still problematic.
They would flare on and off, never fully healing before
flaring again.
This cycle went on for a very long time, but compared to
before, it was manageable.
Anything was a bonus after what I had just been through.
The constant torture of Topical Steroid Withdrawal
(TSW) was behind me.
And even though I still had lingering issues, I was no
longer in pure survival mode.
I could finally function again.

7:14. Wanting Off Methotrexate - The First Step Down

After a year and a half on Methotrexate, I started feeling
the urge to come off it.
I was done with weekly injections.
I was tired of relying on medication.
I wanted to see if my skin could hold up on its own.
At my next hospital appointment, I suggested the idea.
The doctors agreed, but they didn't want me stopping
suddenly.
So we took the first step.

Reducing my dose from 25mg to 15mg.
I was nervous.
What if I flared again?
What if my skin couldn't handle it?
But the weeks passed,
And nothing happened.
No major flare.
No aggressive rebound.
No sudden regression.
My skin held steady.
And for the first time in years,
I finally started to believe that I was healing. And as the weeks went on, I just continued to get better, after all the years of hell I was recovering, I was returning to normality, and showing all the disbelievers, I was correct, and topical steroid withdrawal (TSW) is REAL.

7:15. 2018: The Year Everything Changed

By 2018, I was two years into Topical Steroid Withdrawal (TSW) - and my life had already been torn apart.
But nothing could prepare me for what came next.
My marriage had finally broken down.
Nineteen years together, gone.
I had spent so long fighting my body, trying to hold everything together.

But in the end, it wasn't just my skin that Topical Steroid

Withdrawal (TSW) had destroyed, it had taken everything else with it too.

When I look back, I can't pretend that Topical Steroid Withdrawal (TSW) was the only reason my marriage failed.

Relationships don't fall apart overnight, but there's no doubt in my mind that Topical Steroid Withdrawal (TSW) played a massive part in its downfall.

This condition had stolen so much from me:

Loss of earnings - I had been unable to work for months at a time.

Loss of self-respect - I no longer felt like a man, no longer felt like a provider.

Destruction of my mental health - The suffering had left me broken, isolated, and angry at the world.

The loss of my family - And this? This was the hardest blow of all.

Topical Steroid Withdrawal (TSW) didn't just damage my body, it took everything I had built, everything I cared about, and ripped it apart piece by piece.

And there was nothing I could do to get any of it back.

7:16. The Added Stress - The Flares Return

As my marriage crumbled, I noticed something else happening.

My hands started flaring again.

Was it just a coincidence?

Or was stress triggering another setback?

I believe it was the latter.

We already know that stress is a huge trigger for inflammatory conditions.
The body and mind are deeply connected.
And after everything I had been through, my body was still fragile, still vulnerable.
The emotional strain of my marriage ending seemed to ignite old wounds.
This scared me wondering I how bad this was going to get but
It never got like it was before and calmed down quite quick.

7:17. A Purpose Bigger Than My Own Pain

Do I blame Topical Steroid Withdrawal (TSW) for what happened?
Was it the sole reason for my marriage ending?
I don't know.
But what I do know is this,
Topical Steroid Withdrawal (TSW) took so much from me.
And I can't change that.
I can't get back those lost years.
I can't replace what was taken from me.
I can't undo the damage that was done.
But if this book,
Stops even one person from going through what I did
Prevents even one doctor from prescribing steroids carelessly

Saves even one life from being shattered like mine was
Then maybe, just maybe,
Everything I lost won't have been for nothing.
But before I could find meaning in my suffering, I had to
survive the hardest year of my life."

7:18. Pushing Through the Hardest Year

Selling the house felt like the final chapter closing on my
old life.
It was a painful, emotional process, not just losing the
home itself, but everything it represented.
That house had been my family's home.
It had seen years of memories, good and bad.
And now, it was gone.
I had no choice but to move forward, to rebuild from the
ground up.
I bought my own place, a fresh start, but it didn't feel like
one.
Because this wasn't just a change of address,
It was the reality of a new life I never wanted.
Everything had changed.
My marriage was over.
My kids weren't with me every day anymore.
The life I had worked for was nothing like I imagined it
would be.
But this book isn't about that.
This is about Topical Steroid Withdrawal (TSW).
"And so, I kept pushing forward, despite everything.

Despite the losses.

Despite the physical and mental pain.

But after all those years of suffering, was I finally about to turn a corner?"

7:19. 2018 - A Turning Point in My Recovery

Despite everything else falling apart, something was finally going right,
my skin.
By early 2018, I was seeing real, undeniable improvements, not just tiny changes, but major progress.
The extreme redness was long gone.
The swelling was a thing of the past.
The unbearable heat and burning sensation had gone.
The cracking, splitting, and deep fissures were nonexistent,
My skin was no longer fragile, it had regained strength.
No more flaking all over my clothes, furniture, and bedsheets.
The biggest victory?
No more oozing.
I hadn't experienced none of that for over a year.
I could wear clothes comfortably again without them sticking to my skin.
I could move without pain.
I could sit down without feeling like I was being stabbed by my own body.
My life back.

7:20. The Final Step - Getting Off Metoject

As my skin continued to heal, one thought consumed me,
I want off Metoject.
I had been injecting myself every week for years.
I had been relying on this drug for so long, and I hated it.
So at one of my check-ups at Guy's Hospital, I told them:
"I think it's time. I want to stop."
To my relief, they agreed.
But with one final taper, to 7.5mg.
I wasn't thrilled, but I understood.
They wanted to be cautious, to avoid any sudden flares that could undo all my progress.
I accepted their plan.
At the same time, they told me,
"We think Canterbury can take over your care again."

"We've done everything we can for you."

"You've come such a long way."
This was huge.
After everything I had been through, after years of being treated like a problem patient,
I was finally being told I had made it to the other side.

7:21. Praising Guy's Hospital -The Ones Who Listened

I have nothing but respect for the dermatology team at Guy's Hospital.
Unlike so many other doctors before them.
They listened to me.
They respected my choices.
They didn't dismiss my suffering or force me back onto steroids.
They worked with me, not against me.
They were the first medical professionals who genuinely tried to help me rather than just push the standard treatments and ignore my reality.
I will always be grateful for that.
Because without them, I don't know where I'd be.

7:22. Back to Canterbury - A Step I Wasn't Excited About

I won't lie,
I wasn't exactly thrilled about going back to Canterbury Hospital.
After everything I had been through there, after the years of frustration, dismissal, and being treated like I was insane for questioning steroids, it felt like a step backward.
But at the same time, I knew I should still attend my appointments while I was tapering off Methotrexate.

233

I wanted to be cautious.

I wanted to do this the right way.

When I walked into my first Canterbury appointment after all these years, I could see the shock on their faces. This was not the same broken, red, swollen, oozing man they had last seen.

I didn't look like a severe case anymore.

There wasn't a single blemish on my skin.

I was finally proof that stopping steroids, despite everything they had told me, had been the right choice. And yet,

No apologies.

No acknowledgment of how wrong they had been.

No interest in learning about my journey.

They simply carried on as if none of it had happened.

I didn't let it bother me.

I wasn't there to argue anymore.

I was winning this battle, and that was enough for me.

7:23. Stopping Methotrexate - The Final Step

After a few months on the lower 7.5mg dose, I made the decision,

I wanted off this drug.

I had been injecting myself every week for three years, and I was done.

My skin was the best it had ever looked.

I wasn't flaring anymore.

The risk of infection was lower.

The deep cracks and fissures had healed.

I told Canterbury I was stopping the Methotrexate completely.

They didn't argue.

And just like that, after years of medications, treatments, and constant hospital visits,

I was free.

7:24. Sunbeds - A Surprising Final Boost In Healing

A couple of months after stopping Methotrexate, I decided to experiment with sunbeds.

I had read a lot about how controlled UV exposure could help people with chronic skin conditions, so I thought, Why not try?

I started with just 3 minutes, twice a week.

And within weeks,

my skin had never looked better.

7:25. The Benefits of Sunbeds (If Used Correctly)

While excessive sunbed use is dangerous, when used correctly and in moderation, it can provide huge benefits for skin health, especially for people recovering from severe conditions like Topical Steroid Withdrawal (TSW), eczema, and psoriasis.

Boosts Vitamin D - UV exposure helps your body produce vitamin D, which plays a crucial role in skin health, immune function, and reducing inflammation.

Reduces Inflammation - Controlled exposure to UV light has been shown to suppress the overactive immune response, which is often what causes extreme itching, redness, and flares in conditions like Topical Steroid Withdrawal (TSW).

Improves Skin Barrier Function - Sunbeds increase the production of ceramides, which are natural lipids that help keep the skin barrier strong and prevent water loss, a major issue for Topical Steroid Withdrawal (TSW) sufferers.

Encourages Collagen Production - UV exposure in moderation can help stimulate collagen, which improves skin elasticity and helps heal deep cracks, fissures, and thinning skin.

Helps With Hyperpigmentation & Redness - Topical Steroid Withdrawal (TSW) often leaves patchy redness and uneven skin tone. Sunbeds can help even this out over time, making the skin look more uniform.

Mild Antimicrobial Effect - Sunlight and UV exposure can help kill bacteria on the skin, which lowers the risk of infections, something that had been a huge concern for me throughout Topical Steroid Withdrawal (TSW).

Of course, it's all about balance.
Too much UV exposure can lead to skin damage, premature aging, and even skin cancer.
But small, controlled doses can work wonders for skin recovery.
I made sure to:

Use the lowest possible time setting (starting with 3 minutes)

only go twice a week, never overdoing it.

Moisturise properly afterward to keep my skin from drying out.

Monitor how my skin reacted and adjust accordingly.

And the results were undeniable.

My complexion looked even.

The redness in my face faded. (I think my face will always better redder now than it was before steroid use)

The deep, aggressive flares never came back.

I felt more confident in my own skin than I had in years.

For the first time in over a decade, I felt like a normal person again.

The nightmare of Topical Steroid Withdrawal (TSW) was finally behind me.

No more crippling flares.

No more sleepless, itchy nights.

No more feeling like a prisoner in my own body.

I had been through hell and back, but I had survived.

And now?

I was living proof that healing was possible.

Chapter 8. A New Chapter - Moving To Sweden

8:01. The World Changed

Then, everything shifted.
COVID hit.
Everything slowed down.
At the university, work became quiet, almost pointless.
- The majority of students had gone home.
- With fewer people around, nothing was really breaking down.
- Days dragged on, empty and repetitive.
The job had served its purpose through my worst years.
- It gave me stability when I was at my lowest.
- It allowed me to work when my body was still struggling.
- It gave me space to recover without the stress of a demanding role.
But after seven years,
I needed a change.

8:02. A Big Move: Becoming an Electrical Manager in Sweden

I started looking for new opportunities, something that would challenge me again.

Then, I found it.

A job opening for an Electrical Manager on a new-build data centre in Sweden.

- A big step up from what I was doing.
- A chance to use my skills again.
- A fresh start after everything I'd been through.

I applied.

I got the job.

I was moving to Sweden.

A new country. A new role. A new life.

8:03. Leaving Home: A Tough Decision

The job was based in Sandviken, a small industrial town in Gävleborg County, about 190 km north of Stockholm.

- A quiet place, built around the Sandvik steel company, one of Sweden's oldest manufacturers.
- The town was surrounded by dense forests, lakes, and open countryside, very different from what I was used to.
- Winters were long, dark, and freezing, with snow covering the ground for months.
- Summers, though short, were beautiful, with endless daylight and the famous Swedish "midnight sun" effect.

I would be there full-time.

- I would fly back every third weekend for four days to see my children.

It was a hard decision to make.

I had already lost so much time with them because of

Topical Steroid Withdrawal (TSW).
Now, I was choosing to be away again.
But I knew,
I needed this for myself.
I needed to push forward.
I had spent years stuck in survival mode, just existing.
Now, it was time to live again.

8:04. Worries About My Skin: Would Sweden Make It Worse?

Before the move, I had one big concern.
How would my skin react?
I was still having phone appointments with Canterbury Hospital, but by this point, they felt pointless.
- My skin was stable.
- I hadn't had a major flare in a long time.
- I was barely using any products, just Cetraben and Sudocrem.
Still, I couldn't help but wonder,
would the colder climate trigger something?
Would the stress of moving cause a flare?
Would I be back to square one?
But Sweden surprised me.
- My skin stayed good. - No sudden flares. - No major setbacks. For the first time in years, I felt normal.

8:05. A New Skin Issue: Sweating & Blistering Hands

There was one problem, though.
My hands.
Whenever it got hot, my hands would sweat more than usual.
If they got clammy, small blisters would start to form.
Then the itching would kick in.
It wasn't a major flare, but it was annoying.
- Just another reminder that my skin would never be completely the same again.
Still, after everything I had been through,
this was nothing.

8:06. A Special Holiday - Taking My Kids to Turkey

In 2022, I did something I had been dreaming of for years,
I took two of my children on holiday.
We went to Lara Beach, Antalya, Turkey.
Lara Beach is known as the "Las Vegas" of Turkey,
- Five-star, all-inclusive resorts stretch along the golden coastline.
- The Mediterranean Sea is warm and crystal-clear, perfect for swimming.
- The area is famous for its extravagant hotels, each designed to look like something different, one shaped like

the Titanic, another like a Venetian palace.

- The food, the entertainment, the beach, it was everything a perfect holiday should be.

For the first time in years, I felt like a normal dad.

- Waking up in a luxury resort, having breakfast by the sea.

- Watching my kids laugh, splash in the pools, and just enjoy life.

- Sitting on the beach in the warm Turkish sun, feeling grateful to be here.

The heat was intense.

And, as expected,

my hands reacted only slightly.

- The sweat made them itch.

- The humidity caused small flare-ups.

But I didn't care.

I was on holiday with my kids having the best time.

A couple from our trip to Turkey, finally free from Topical Steroid withdrawal

8:07. An Unexpected Connection: Meeting Someone in Turkey

While we were staying at the hotel, I got talking to one of the staff.
There was something about her,
- We clicked straight away.
- Conversations flowed easily.
- We got to know each other a bit in the last two days of that trip.
She was Kurdish Turkish, working at the hotel in Antalya.

After I left, we kept in touch.
And over the next year and a half,
I found myself flying to Turkey once a month to see her.
Life was good at this point.

My skin was stable.
I was working abroad, using my skills again.
I was travelling, meeting new people, living again.
For the first time in nearly a decade,
I felt like me.

8:08. A Trip to Adana: Experiencing the Real Heat of Turkey

In July 2023, Zehra and I planned a trip to Adana, her hometown.
We was attending a Zehra's friend's wedding.
We would also visit her family for a few days.
This wasn't just a small trip, it was my first time experiencing the southern heat of Turkey.
I had spent time in Antalya before, but Adana was on another level.
What is Adana Like?
Adana is one of Turkey's largest cities, located in the southern region near the Mediterranean.
It's known for its incredibly hot summers, one of the hottest places in the country.
The city sits along the Seyhan River, with stunning old bridges and a mix of modern and traditional architecture.
It's famous for Adana Kebab, a spiced, grilled meat dish loved across Turkey.
The culture is heavily influenced by both Turkish and Arabic traditions, making it a unique part of the country.

Before I went, I had heard stories about Adana's heat.
People said it could drive you crazy.
There's even a famous story about a man trying to shoot down the sun because it was too hot.
At first, I thought that was just an exaggeration.
Then I stepped off the plane,
It was like stepping into an oven.
Even the air felt heavy, thick, and almost suffocating.

There was no escaping the heat, it clung to you, even in the shade.

This wasn't the kind of dry heat I had felt in other places. This was a humid, sticky heat, the kind that made your clothes cling to your skin and left you constantly searching for the nearest air-conditioned building.

I had been in hot places before, but nothing like this.

8:09. A Small Flare-Up: My Hands Reacting to the Heat

By this point in my journey, my skin was doing well.

No flares.

But my hands had always been a weak spot.

In extreme heat, my hands would sweat more than usual.

When they got too clammy, small blisters would start to appear.

It was nothing like before,

No unbearable itch.

No deep cracks.

No constant suffering.

It was just annoying.

A minor flare-up, but still frustrating, especially when I was enjoying my time away.

That's when Zehra decided to take action.

Before I could even settle in, she had already booked me in with a doctor.

8:10. Straight to the Doctor: The Turkish Healthcare System in Action

I had barely been in Adana for two hours when Zehra took me straight to her family doctor. Her mum worked at the clinic, so she pulled some strings. The doctor immediately arranged for me to see a dermatologist. Within a couple of hours, I had seen a doctor and I was sitting in the dermatologist's office.

I couldn't believe how quickly it all happened, hours, not months. Back in England, I'd have waited weeks just for a referral, let alone a specialist. So why was Turkey so much faster? It comes down to a system built for action. Since 2003.

Turkey's Health Transformation Program turned a sluggish, centralised setup into something nimble. They rolled out universal health insurance, streamlined appointments with tools like the MHRS system, a hotline or app that books you in fast, and poured resources into accessible care. In a city like Adana, with private and public clinics working side by side, competition keeps things moving. Plus, Zehra's mum pulling strings at the clinic didn't hurt, personal connections can cut through red tape anywhere, but here they paired with a system already primed for speed. In England, I was a number in a queue; in Turkey, I was a patient they couldn't wait to help.

8:11. Hand Botox - A Treatment I Had Never Heard Of

I went in to see the dermatologist and she listened to my story and seemed to know all about topical steroid withdrawal (TSW) and showed her pictures of what I had been through and explained that this is just a slight niggle to what I have been through and I'm not majorly concerned, but it is still annoying.

After listening to my full history, the dermatologist nodded and said:
"Have you ever considered Botox for your hands?"
Botox? In my hands?
I had never even heard of Botox for hands before.
She explained that Botox injections could stop excessive sweating.
- It blocks the nerves that trigger the sweat glands.
- If my hands didn't sweat, I wouldn't get blisters.
- If I didn't get blisters, I wouldn't get flare-ups.
It made sense.
And after everything I had been through, I was willing to try it.
But. I had no idea what I had just signed up for.

8:12. The Botox Procedure - A Painful Experience

They put some numbing gel on both my hands why the nurse prepared the injections.

- It was Botulinum Toxin A, the same stuff people use for wrinkles.

- But instead of foreheads and frown lines, it was going straight into my palms.

The Process:

1 They then cleaned my hands with antiseptic.

2 Marked injection points across my palms and fingers.

3 Began injecting tiny amounts of Botox into each spot.

It was so painful.

Like really painful!!

- Dozens of injections in each hand.

- Each one felt like a deep, burning stab.

- I gritted my teeth, gripping the chair. Why Zehra is rubbing my head and trying her best not to laugh at me in pain.

I didn't scream, but fuck, I wanted to.

Luckily, the pain didn't last long once the injections were done.

8:13. The Results - Did It Work?

100% YES.

-My hands didn't sweat all summer.

- No sweating meant no blisters.

- No blisters meant no irritation.

For the first time in years, my hands felt completely normal.

Even in 40°C heat, I had zero issues.

No itching.

No peeling.

No discomfort.

Would I do it again?

- Yes.

Was it painful?

- Absolutely.

Did it solve my problem?

- Completely.

The only downside?

- The effects wear off after a few months, so it's not permanent.

But for a summer with lots of trips to Turkey planned, it was exactly what I needed.

Topical Steroid Withdrawal (TSW) had taken so much from me over the years.

But this?

This was an actual solution.

It wasn't a cure, but it was a fix for a problem that had plagued me for years.

And after everything I had been through?
I will continue with the hand Botox at the start of every summer, it will give me peace of mind.

Ryan Thomson
The Eczema Deception

Left photo is my hands immediately after the 2nd lot of Botox. Right photo is my hand currently, no issues whatsoever, Healing happens!!

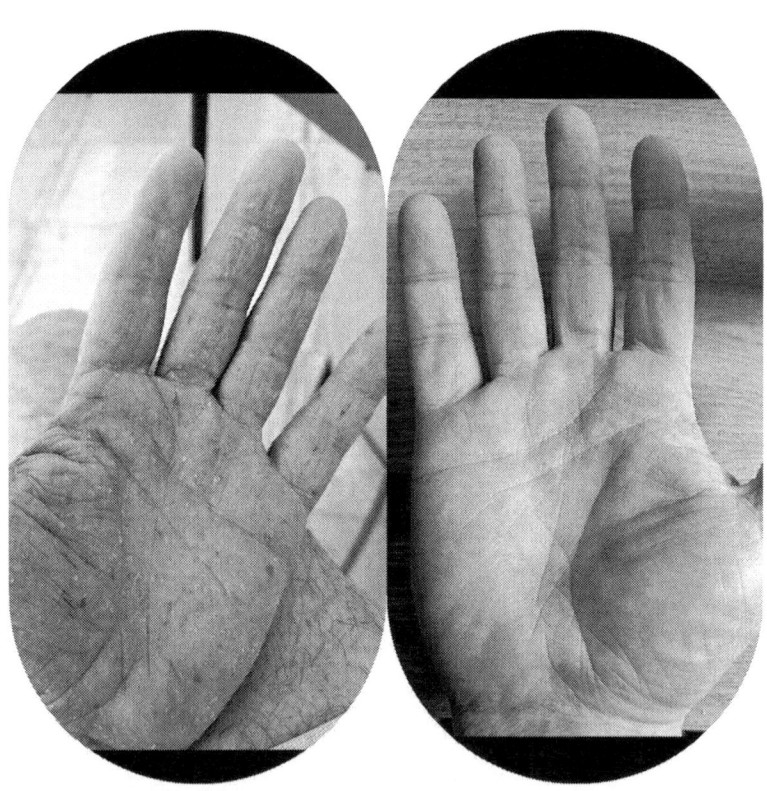

Chapter 9. My Life Now

9:01. The End of the Road

As I sit here in Frankfurt, Germany, reflecting on the last decade, I can finally say, I made it through.

- I've been here for 18 months, still working in data centres, still building a life.

- My skin is good. Not just better, not just manageable, back to normal.

- The suffering that once consumed every second of my life is gone.

I had hand Botox redone last summer and will do it again this year.

It's a cheap, simple fix, a way to guarantee I won't deal with the heat-induced irritation that once bothered my hands.

A small thing. A small inconvenience. But after everything I've been through, it's nothing.

9:02. A Body That's Been Through War

I still think about what my body has endured.
I still wonder about the damage, the long-term effects, and the trauma.
I spent years throwing every treatment imaginable at my skin.

Not just steroids, but strong, heavy-duty, systemic medications designed to suppress my immune system and force my body into submission.

Here's what my body has been through:

- Azathioprine - an immunosuppressant, used for organ transplant patients, to stop the immune system from attacking itself.

- Ciclosporin - another powerful immunosuppressant, often used for severe psoriasis.

- Toctino (Alitretinoin) - a potent retinoid, known for its harsh side effects.

- Prednisone - an oral steroid that wreaks havoc on your body, causing dependency and withdrawal.

- Methotrexate (Metoject) - a chemotherapy drug, used in lower doses to suppress inflammation.

- Topical steroids of all strengths, from mild to the most potent, lathered onto my skin for years, without warning of the consequences.

That's what it took for my body to finally break.

That's what led me down the road to hell, Topical Steroid Withdrawal.

What's Left Behind - The Lingering Questions

My skin is strong again.

My body has recovered.

But still, there's a part of me that wonders.

What damage has been done on the inside?

What will the long-term effects of these medications be?

Will my immune system ever be what it was before?

That's why I'm doing full blood work in Germany,

I want to know for sure that I'm healthy.

I want to see with my own eyes that my body has made it through intact.

Because even though I feel good, even though my skin is healed,
I still carry the weight of years of medical abuse,
and I need to know if it left invisible scars.

Moving Forward - Where Do I Go from Here?
I don't know how long I'll stay in Germany.
Maybe I'll move on, maybe I won't.
But wherever I go, one thing is certain, I will never go back to that life.
All I want now is to live.
To try and get my children back in my life, some people was not happy with me meeting Zehra and that led to me losing all contact with my children for over 2 years now, which breaks my heart daily. But they know I am always there for them when they are ready.

To travel and experience life without the fear of my skin holding me back.
The road to healing was long, so, so brutal, and unforgiving.
But I walked it.
I made it to the other side.
I'm free.
And for the first time in years, I can finally say,
I'm just me again, but with a lot less than when I started this journey. It's taken a hell of a lot from me and has a lot to answer for.
That I can never forgive the doctors, dermatologists and pharmaceutical companies for.

And I can never recuperate any of those losses, I can earn money again but I can't replace my stable life and family, no money can replace that. That's gone for good. But I will keep pushing on.

Enjoying life again, paddle boarding on Konyaalti Antalya

From what I went through to this was crazy a journey. And one that I hope can help someone.

Chapter 10. Treatments

10:01. Treatments That Helped Me - And What I Wish I Had Known Earlier

Topical Steroid Withdrawal (TSW) is relentless. There are no quick fixes, no miracle creams, no prescribed solutions that make it all go away. The only real cure is time.

But that doesn't mean there's no relief to be found along the way.

Through trial and error, and a lot of suffering, I found treatments that eased the symptoms, calmed the burning, soothed the itch, and gave me moments of peace.

Some treatments were simple, natural remedies; others were prescribed by doctors; and some I stumbled across through other sufferers in online support groups.

This part is not about false hope.

It's about practical, real solutions that helped me, and that might help others still deep in this nightmare.

I have mentioned some of these in the book but created a go to part if you need quick relief.

10:02. The Treatments That Helped Me Through Topical Steroid Withdrawal (TSW)

1. Epsom Salt Baths - The Only True Relief I Had
If I could have lived in the bath, I would have.
When the burning, itching, and tightness of my skin became too much, Epsom salt baths were the only thing that brought immediate relief.
What are they?
Epsom salts are magnesium sulphate, and when dissolved in warm water, they help with inflammation, muscle relaxation, and detoxification.

How they helped me:
- Instantly reduced the deep itch and burning
- Relaxed my body, helping me mentally reset
- Loosened stiff, cracked, and thickened skin

- Helped dry out oozing wounds

- Improved my circulation and reduced swelling

How I used them:
- Twice a day (morning and night)
- Warm water, not hot (hot water made the skin worse)
- A few drops of tea tree oil mixed in for antibacterial benefits
- Soaked for 15-30 minutes, then applied moisturisers immediately

The downside:

- Relief was temporary - as soon as I stepped out, the symptoms crept back

- Too much soaking made my skin prune and dry out

Would I recommend it?

YES. If you have Topical Steroid Withdrawal (TSW) and haven't tried Epsom salt baths, you're missing out on one of the best natural ways to manage symptoms.

2. Tea Tree Oil - A Natural Antiseptic That Kept Me from Infection

Small but powerful.

I added a few drops of tea tree oil into my Epsom salt baths, and it helped keep my open skin clean and infection-free.

What is it?

Tea tree oil is a natural antiseptic with antibacterial, antifungal, and anti-inflammatory properties.

How it helped me:

- Helped prevent infections in broken skin

- Dried up oozing areas faster

- Reduced swelling and irritation

How I used it:

- Diluted in my bath water (never directly on raw skin)

- Mixed a few drops into my moisturiser

The downside:

- Too strong undiluted - applying directly burned like hell
- Could be drying - too much made my skin feel tight

Would I recommend it?
YES, but always diluted.

3. Sudocrem - The Best Barrier for Open Skin.
A thick, protective layer for my worst wounds.

What is it?
Sudocrem is a zinc oxide-based cream originally meant for nappy rash, but it works wonders for cracked, raw, or broken skin.

How it helped me:

- Created a protective barrier over painful cracks
- Helped calm irritation and redness
- Slightly numbed the most painful spots
- Promoted faster healing of splits in my hands and feet

The downside:

- Thick and messy - stuck to clothes and sheets
- Not ideal for large areas - best for targeted application

Would I recommend it?
Yes, for cracked and open wounds.

4. Jojoba Oil - The Game-Changer for My Face
The first thing that made my face feel normal again.

What is Jojoba Oil?

Jojoba oil is a liquid wax that closely mimics the skin's natural sebum, making it one of the best oils for moisturising without clogging pores.

How it helped me:

- Hydrated my face without irritation
- Balanced oil production - helped with dryness and redness
- Didn't feel greasy, absorbed easily

The downside:

- Expensive compared to basic moisturisers
- Didn't work well on deep cracks, only surface-level relief

Would I recommend it?

Absolutely, especially for facial recovery.

5. Bleach Baths - Strange, But Effective.

A controversial treatment, but it worked for me.

Why I tried it:

Dermatologists at Guy's Hospital recommended using Milton Fluid (baby bottle steriliser) in my baths to prevent infections.

How it helped me:

- Kept open wounds cleaner
- Helped stop staph infections from forming
- Reduced red, inflamed patches

The downside:

- Made my skin drier.
- The idea of bathing in bleach was unsettling.

Would I recommend it?

Yes, but in moderation.

6. Hand Botox - The Best Fix for Heat-Induced Flares
Something I wish I had known about sooner.

Why I tried it:
In hot weather, my hands would sweat excessively,
leading to blisters and flare-ups.
A dermatologist in Turkey suggested Botox injections in
my hands to stop the sweating.

How it helped me:

- Completely stopped sweating in my hands for months
- Prevented heat-triggered blisters
- No more irritation from clammy skin

The downside:

- EXTREMELY painful - felt like hundreds of needles
- Needs to be repeated every few months

Would I recommend it? If sweating triggers your flares,
YES.

6. Cetraben, my favourite moisturiser, I still keep a bottle
of this always at home.

Final Thoughts - What I Wish I Had Known Sooner
If I could go back in time, what would I tell myself?

- Stop steroids sooner - I wasted years trusting doctors who didn't understand the damage they were causing.
- Find a dermatologist who listens - The right doctor can make all the difference.
- Natural solutions work - Not everything needs to come from a prescription pad.
- Healing takes time - There's no quick fix, but there is relief along the way.

Would I change what I went through?
If it meant warning others before it was too late, maybe not.
Because if sharing my story stops even one person from suffering like I did,
Then maybe everything I went through wasn't for nothing.

10:03. Treatments I Wish I Had Tried Sooner - And Why They Could Have Helped

Looking back, there are treatments I now know about that could have made a huge difference if I had used them earlier.
Topical Steroid Withdrawal (TSW) is unpredictable, what works for one person might not work for another, but these are treatments backed by science and real-world

experiences that could have sped up healing, reduced inflammation, or made the suffering more manageable.

1. Red Light Therapy - Could Have Reduced Inflammation & Helped Skin Repair

Topical Steroid Withdrawal (TSW) is all about inflammation. The body is in a constant state of distress, and the skin's barrier is completely compromised.

What is Red Light Therapy?

Red light therapy (RLT) uses low-wavelength red light to penetrate deep into the skin, helping to: -- Reduce inflammation - Calms the overactive immune response
- Boost collagen production - Supports skin regeneration and repair
- Improve circulation - Helps bring oxygen and nutrients to damaged skin
- Speed up wound healing - Proven to help eczema and psoriasis

Why I Wish I Had Used It:

At my worst, my skin wasn't just dry, it was broken, raw, and constantly flaring. If I had started red light therapy early on, it could have:

- Shortened my recovery time

- Helped repair deep cracks and fissures

- Reduced the extreme redness and swelling

- Boosted my skin's ability to heal itself

The Downside:

- It can be expensive to get a high-quality red light panel

265

- Needs consistent use to see real benefits
Would I recommend it?
Yes, especially for people still deep in Topical Steroid
Withdrawal (TSW) or those struggling with stubborn
flares.

2. Zinc & Vitamin C - The Power Duo for Skin Repair
Nutrition matters more than people realise. When the
skin is in crisis, it needs the right nutrients to heal, and
zinc and vitamin C are two of the most important ones.
Why These Nutrients Matter:
- Zinc is essential for skin regeneration - It speeds up
wound healing and reduces inflammation
- Vitamin C is crucial for collagen production - It
strengthens the skin's barrier and helps repair damaged
tissue

Why I Wish I Had Taken Them Sooner:
- I had open wounds and cracks for months, zinc could
have sped up healing
- My skin's barrier was completely broken, vitamin C
could have helped rebuild it
- Topical Steroid Withdrawal (TSW) leads to nutrient
depletion, I likely had low zinc levels without realising it

The Downside:
- Too much zinc can cause nausea, best to take it with
food
- Vitamin C alone won't fix skin damage, needs to be
part of an overall nutrition strategy

Would I recommend it?
Absolutely, these are two of the best vitamins for skin healing.

3. Collagen Supplements - Could Have Supported Barrier Repair & Elasticity

Topical Steroid Withdrawal (TSW) destroys the skin's structure? It causes thinning, tearing, and premature aging, which means the body needs extra help rebuilding lost collagen.

What is Collagen?
Collagen is the main protein that gives skin its strength, structure, and elasticity.

How It Could Have Helped Me:
- Strengthened my skin barrier - making it more resistant to cracks and flares
- Promoted elasticity - helping the skin return to normal faster
- Reduced scarring - could have improved areas that were constantly damaged
- Improved hydration - collagen helps skin retain moisture, which is critical for Topical Steroid Withdrawal (TSW) recovery

Why I Wish I Had Taken It Sooner:
- My skin was paper-thin for months, collagen might have helped restore its thickness
- Repeated cracking and tearing slowed my progress, collagen could have helped prevent deep fissures

- Topical Steroid Withdrawal (TSW) leads to rapid collagen breakdown, taking it might have helped maintain skin integrity

The Downside:
- It takes weeks to months to see results
- Not all collagen supplements are effective, some are poorly absorbed
Would I recommend it?
Yes, especially for long-term skin barrier recovery.

4. Oat Baths - A Simple, Soothing Treatment I Overlooked
Oats are one of nature's best skin healers. I used Epsom salts, but I never tried colloidal oatmeal baths, which might have offered a different type of relief.
What Makes Oats Special?
- Contain beta-glucans - naturally anti-inflammatory and soothing
- Help lock in moisture - crucial for preventing dry, cracked skin
- Reduce itching and irritation - often used for eczema sufferers

Why I Wish I Had Used Them:
- Could have cooled my burning skin without being too drying
- Might have helped with swelling and soothed tight, inflamed areas
- Would have given me another bath option besides

Epsom salts

The Downside:
- Can get messy, oats clog drains if not used properly
- May not be strong enough for severe cases
Would I recommend it?
Yes, for those still experiencing itch and dryness.

5. Adaptogens (Ashwagandha & Rhodiola) - Could Have Helped Manage Stress & Cortisol Levels
Topical Steroid Withdrawal (TSW) is not just a skin condition, it's a full-body stress response. The extreme stress causes high cortisol levels, which in turn worsen inflammation and prolong healing.

What Are Adaptogens?
Adaptogens are natural herbs that help the body regulate stress hormones and improve resilience.

The Best Ones for Topical Steroid Withdrawal (TSW):
- Ashwagandha - Helps lower cortisol, improve sleep, and reduce anxiety
- Rhodiola Rosea - Helps with energy levels, mood, and adrenal fatigue

Why I Wish I Had Used Them:
- Chronic stress worsens skin conditions, adaptogens could have helped calm my nervous system
- I had months of insomnia, Ashwagandha might have helped me sleep better

- My energy levels were completely drained, Rhodiola could have helped me push through recovery

The Downside:
- Can take a few weeks to work
- Some people react differently, best to start slow
Would I recommend it? Yes, especially for managing stress during Topical Steroid Withdrawal (TSW).

6. Magnesium Glycinate - Could Have Helped Me Sleep
Sleep deprivation was one of the worst parts of Topical Steroid Withdrawal (TSW). Magnesium could have made a difference.

Why is Magnesium Important?
- Regulates the nervous system - helps with relaxation and deep sleep
- Reduces muscle cramps - might have helped with restless, twitching legs
- Calms the skin - has a natural anti-inflammatory effect

Why I Wish I Had Taken It Sooner:
I went months without proper sleep, magnesium might have helped reset my sleep cycle
- My stress levels were through the roof, magnesium naturally lowers anxiety
- My skin was constantly inflamed, magnesium could have reduced cortisol levels

The Downside:

- Takes a few weeks to see full benefits
- Too much can cause digestive issues

Would I recommend it?

YES, this is one of the best, safest supplements for sleep and stress.

Final Thoughts on What I Wish I Had Tried

I can't go back and change my journey. But I can share this knowledge to help others.

If you're going through Topical Steroid Withdrawal (TSW), experiment. Try different approaches. Find what works for you.

Because every bit of relief, no matter how small, makes this nightmare just a little easier to bear.

Chapter 11. The Denial

CHAPTER 11:01 Why Doctors Won't Admit Topical Steroid Withdrawal (TSW) IS REAL

By now, you've read my journey. You've seen the suffering, the isolation, the complete breakdown of my body and mind. And if you've been through anything similar, you might have asked yourself the same question I did, time and time again:

Why do doctors refuse to acknowledge that Topical Steroid Withdrawal (TSW) is real?

Why did I have to fight for years to be heard?

Why was I dismissed as non-compliant, as stubborn, as reckless, when all I was doing was trying to break free from the very treatment that had destroyed me?

Why was I gaslit, ignored, and passed from one dermatologist to another, all while they continued pushing the same drugs that had left me in ruins?

The truth is brutal.

Doctors won't admit that Topical Steroid Withdrawal (TSW) is real because the entire medical system is built on pharmaceutical trust, outdated textbooks, and an unwillingness to question decades of standard practice.

And if they do acknowledge it?

If they accept that Topical Steroid Withdrawal (TSW) exists?

Then they are forced to admit that they have harmed thousands, maybe millions, of patients, whether they meant to or not.

This chapter isn't just about my personal frustration with doctors. This is about the systemic failure that has led to an entire epidemic of people suffering in silence.

11:02. The Role of Medical Textbooks - If It's Not in the Books, It's Not in Their Minds

To understand why doctors, refuse to recognise Topical Steroid Withdrawal (TSW), we have to start with their education.

Medical professionals are trained using approved medical textbooks, rigorously peer-reviewed, but also slow to evolve. These books dictate what doctors learn, what conditions they recognise, and what treatments they prescribe.

And guess what?

Topical Steroid Withdrawal (TSW) isn't in those textbooks.

Not in dermatology reference books.

Not in medical school curricula.

Not in the standard guidelines used to diagnose and treat skin conditions.

Instead, these books present topical steroids as a gold standard for treating eczema, psoriasis, and other inflammatory skin diseases. They are described as safe when used "appropriately," and the withdrawal effects are completely ignored.

Doctors are trained to believe in steroids as the solution, not as the cause of a deeper problem.

So when a patient like me walks into a dermatology clinic, covered in red, burning, oozing skin, insisting that steroids have destroyed their body, a doctor cannot compute it.

It doesn't match what they were taught.

And in the medical world, if it's not in the books, it's not real.

This is why so many dermatologists double down when a patient brings up Topical Steroid Withdrawal (TSW).

Instead of considering that steroids may be causing long-term damage, they assume the patient has severe eczema, psoriasis, or atopic dermatitis that needs stronger treatment.

This is exactly why so many of us get prescribed even more steroids or get pushed onto immunosuppressants like methotrexate, ciclosporin, or Dupixent.

If doctors admit that Topical Steroid Withdrawal (TSW) exists, they also have to admit that the very drugs they have spent their entire careers prescribing might be doing long-term harm.

And for most of them, that's simply too big a pill to swallow.

11:03. The Pharmaceutical Industry - Profits Over Patients

The refusal to acknowledge Topical Steroid Withdrawal (TSW) doesn't just come from outdated textbooks. It comes from money.

274

The pharmaceutical industry relies on chronic illness to maintain its profits.

Topical steroids are a billion-dollar industry.

Eczema alone affects over 200 million people worldwide.

Most patients are given topical steroids as a first-line treatment.

Many are never told about the risks of long-term use. And when those steroids start causing dependence, withdrawal, and worsening flares, what happens?

Patients keep going back to dermatologists for stronger prescriptions, additional medications, and expensive treatments.

It's a perfect cycle of dependence, one that keeps patients locked in a lifetime of managing symptoms rather than actually curing the problem.

The pharmaceutical industry benefits immensely from this.

They sell steroids for the initial eczema diagnosis. When they stop working, they push stronger steroids or switch the patient to immunosuppressants. When the immune system becomes compromised, they sell antibiotics, antifungals, and other secondary treatments.

And here's the most sinister part:

If Topical Steroid Withdrawal (TSW) was widely acknowledged, it could destroy the entire business model that dermatology is built on.

If patients knew that their worsening skin wasn't their eczema getting worse, but actually their body reacting to steroid withdrawal, then they would stop using steroids altogether.

And the moment that happens, pharmaceutical companies lose a lifelong customer.

Is this why there is no funding for large-scale Topical Steroid Withdrawal (TSW) research?

Is this why mainstream dermatology organisations don't warn patients about it?

Is this why doctors are trained to dismiss Topical Steroid Withdrawal (TSW) as an internet conspiracy rather than investigate it seriously?

Because there is no profit in healing.

There is only profit in managing symptoms forever.

11:04. Why Dermatologists Will Never Admit Fault

Even if a dermatologist suspects that a patient's skin damage is due to Topical Steroid Withdrawal (TSW), they will never admit it outright.

Why?

Because the moment they do, they are legally and ethically responsible.

If a doctor officially recognises Topical Steroid Withdrawal (TSW), then they must also acknowledge that they have been prescribing a harmful treatment for years.

That means:

- They have misdiagnosed potentially thousands of patients.

- They have caused severe, life-altering side effects.

- They could face legal consequences for medical malpractice.

So instead of taking responsibility, most dermatologists deny, deflect, and gaslight patients into compliance. They blame the patient for not using steroids correctly. They say that withdrawal symptoms are just severe eczema flares. They push stronger drugs instead of acknowledging the damage steroids have already done. They protect their reputations over protecting their patients.

And this is why people like me, who have suffered through years of agony, are left feeling like we are the crazy ones.

11:05. The Slow Fight for Recognition

Despite all of this, the truth about Topical Steroid Withdrawal (TSW) is spreading.

Support groups are growing, from a few thousand members in 2014 to tens of thousands today. More doctors are starting to listen, particularly in Japan and the U.S., where small studies have confirmed that steroid withdrawal is real. More patients are refusing steroids, choosing alternative treatments instead.

But it's a slow fight.

Until Topical Steroid Withdrawal (TSW) is recognised in medical textbooks, taught in dermatology training, and acknowledged in official guidelines, we will always be fighting to prove that this condition is real.

And even when the medical community finally

acknowledges Topical Steroid Withdrawal (TSW), there will be no apology. No compensation for those of us who lost years of our lives to it. No justice for the careers, families, and mental health that were destroyed. But if this book can serve one purpose, if it can make one doctor question the system they work in, if it can prevent one patient from suffering like I did, then maybe, just maybe, the fight will have been worth it. Because we deserve better. And the truth will come out Whether they like it or not.

11:06. The Thousands Who Suffer in Silence - And the Doctors Who Refuse to Acknowledge It

 For every person who fights through Topical Steroid Withdrawal (TSW) and comes out the other side, there are thousands more who never even realise what's happening to them.

They sit in a dermatologist's office, desperate for relief, only to be handed another prescription for stronger steroids, immunosuppressant's, or even biologics like Dupixent. They're told, "This will help."

And at first, it does. The inflammation settles, the itching dulls, and for a little while, they believe their doctor was right.

Until the cycle starts again.

The flares return, often worse than before. The skin stops responding to treatment. New, unexplained symptoms emerge, redness that won't fade, burning sensations, relentless itching that no cream or medication can soothe.

They go back to the doctor, confused, trusting that medicine has the answer.

And what happens?

They are gaslit.

They are told their eczema is just "severe" now.

They are blamed for not applying steroids correctly.

They are prescribed something even stronger.

And so, the suffering continues.

For years. For some, their health declines so severely that they lose their jobs, their relationships, and their ability to function in daily life.

Many fall into depression. Some reach a level of despair so deep that they question whether they can survive this. And all the while, doctors refuse to admit what's happening.

They ignore the growing number of patients experiencing the same horrifying withdrawal symptoms. They dismiss the research coming out of Japan, the U.S., and other countries confirming Topical Steroid Withdrawal (TSW) is real. They silence the voices of those who have suffered, healed, and tried to warn others.

Even now, in 2025, most dermatologists still follow the same outdated, pharmaceutical-driven treatment approach:

If steroids stop working, increase the potency. If a patient resists, blame them for non-compliance. If withdrawal symptoms appear, deny that withdrawal exists.

And the cruellest part?

By the time many Topical Steroid Withdrawal (TSW)

sufferers realise what's happening, it's far too late. Their skin is already addicted. Their immune system is already compromised. Their mental health is already shattered.

And they are forced to go through the agonising process of withdrawal without medical support.

Because no doctor wants to be the one to admit that the entire system is broken.

11:07. The Consequences of Medical Negligence

This isn't just a story of personal suffering. This is medical negligence on a global scale. Thousands of people, children, teenagers, adults, are being misdiagnosed, mistreated, and left to suffer alone.

Many lose years of their lives to an avoidable condition. Many develop long-term health issues from immunosuppressant's they never should have needed. Many are permanently traumatised, not just from the physical pain, but from the betrayal of a system they were told to trust.

And still, the medical world refuses to listen.

Imagine a world where: Topical Steroid Withdrawal (TSW) is recognised in medical textbooks. Doctors warn patients about the risk of steroid addiction before prescribing. Dermatologists are trained to wean patients off steroids safely, rather than leaving them to suffer. Pharmaceutical companies prioritise patient safety over profits.

That world should exist. But it doesn't, because admitting the truth would cost too much. And so, we continue to fight alone.

11:08. Will Things Ever Change?

The hard truth? For change to happen, the medical world has to reach a breaking point. A moment where the suffering can no longer be ignored.
Topical Steroid Withdrawal (TSW) has to become too big to deny.
Too many voices have to speak out.
Too much research has to surface.
We are getting closer. But the fight isn't over.
Until then, people like me, people who have been through the worst of it, have to be the ones to tell the truth.
Because if we don't?
Then the next person who walks into a dermatologist's office with a small patch of eczema will leave with a steroid prescription.
And years later, they'll find themselves exactly where I was.
Begging for answers.
Trapped in their own skin.
And completely alone.
We cannot let that happen. The world needs to wake up. And it needs to happen now!!!

Chapter 12. - Spreading Awareness and Moving Forward

12:01 The Future of Topical Steroid Withdrawal (TSW) - Will It Ever Be Recognised Medically?

For decades, Topical Steroid Withdrawal (TSW) has existed in the shadows of dermatology, ignored, denied, and dismissed by mainstream medicine. Even as thousands of people worldwide suffer through identical withdrawal symptoms, the medical establishment continues to act as if Topical Steroid Withdrawal (TSW) is nothing more than an "online theory" or an "uncommon side effect" of steroid misuse.

But is that true? No. The truth is Topical Steroid Withdrawal (TSW) is real, and the evidence is becoming impossible to ignore. So, the question now is: Will Topical Steroid Withdrawal (TSW) ever be fully recognised as a legitimate medical condition? And if so, how long will it take?

12:02. What Needs to Happen for Topical Steroid Withdrawal (TSW) to Be Officially Recognised?

For Topical Steroid Withdrawal (TSW) to be formally acknowledged within the medical community, key things need to happen:

1. Inclusion in Medical Textbooks & Guidelines

Right now, most dermatology textbooks don't mention Topical Steroid Withdrawal (TSW) at all.

If it's not in textbooks, doctors aren't trained to recognise it.

The standard guidelines for treating eczema, dermatitis, and other skin conditions do not warn about long-term steroid use leading to withdrawal.

For Topical Steroid Withdrawal (TSW) to be taken seriously, it needs to be written into medical education materials so that new dermatologists learn about it from the beginning, not just through desperate patients trying to explain it to them.

2. Large-Scale Clinical Studies.

While some research has been done, especially in Japan and the U.S, it's not enough.

The medical world only believes in evidence-based medicine, and for them, that means large-scale clinical trials.

If a drug company wants to get a new treatment approved, they conduct randomised controlled trials (RCTs) with thousands of participants, Topical Steroid

Withdrawal (TSW) needs the same level of research.

The problem?

Who is going to fund those studies?

Pharmaceutical companies won't fund research that exposes the damage caused by their own products. Governments rarely fund research that could lead to expensive lawsuits against the healthcare system.

3. Pressure from the Public & Patient Advocacy Groups.

The medical industry doesn't change unless it's forced to. The only reason conditions like long-COVID, chronic Lyme disease, and even fibromyalgia started getting recognition was because patients refused to be ignored.

Thousands of people had to speak out, share their stories, and demand that doctors take them seriously.

This is exactly what needs to happen with Topical Steroid Withdrawal (TSW).

4. Acknowledgment from Dermatology Associations & Health Authorities

Organisations like the American Academy of Dermatology (AAD), the British Association of Dermatologists (BAD), and the World Health Organisation (WHO) all have a say in what is classified as a real medical condition.

So far, none of these organisations have officially recognised Topical Steroid Withdrawal (TSW).

If they did, it would change everything, because suddenly, doctors would have to acknowledge it in their practice.

For that to happen, scientific evidence and patient demand must reach a tipping point where these organisations can no longer ignore it.

12:03. How Close Are We to That Reality?

Right now, Topical Steroid Withdrawal (TSW) is at a crossroads. It's not a completely unknown condition anymore, thanks to social media, patient groups, and independent researchers, more people are learning about it.

More doctors are privately acknowledging that they've seen Topical Steroid Withdrawal (TSW) in patients.

More patients are sharing their recovery stories.

More dermatologists are starting to question whether long-term steroid use is truly safe.

But the problem remains the same.

The majority of dermatologists still refuse to admit their treatments could be causing harm.

The pharmaceutical industry has too much financial power over medical research.

The official guidelines for treating skin conditions haven't changed in decades.

So, while we are making progress, true recognition is still years away.

12.04. What Could Speed Up the Process?

If we want Topical Steroid Withdrawal (TSW) to be officially recognised faster, we need to apply pressure in every possible way:

More research studies - Scientists and doctors who

understand Topical Steroid Withdrawal (TSW) must push for larger-scale research.

More media exposure - The more newspapers, documentaries, and online news sites that cover Topical Steroid Withdrawal (TSW), the more awareness spreads.

More patient advocacy - Organisations like ITSAN and other skin health groups need to push harder for change.

More public demand - If enough people speak out, governments and health authorities will have no choice but to listen.

12:05. The Harsh Truth: Some Doctors Will Never Admit the Truth

Even when Topical Steroid Withdrawal (TSW) is eventually recognised, there will always be doctors who refuse to believe it.

Some will double down on their denial, refusing to accept that they've spent their careers unknowingly harming patients.

Some will claim that Topical Steroid Withdrawal (TSW) only happens to people who "misuse" steroids, even though thousands of sufferers used them exactly as prescribed.

Some will continue pushing biologics and immunosuppressant's as the next big solution, ignoring the real cause of the problem, skin addiction to steroids.

But for every doctor that refuses to admit the truth, more patients will find the information themselves.

They will see the thousands of other people going

through the same thing.

They will read the personal stories, watch the documentaries, and come across the scientific studies that prove Topical Steroid Withdrawal (TSW) is real.

And eventually, Topical Steroid Withdrawal (TSW) will become so well-known that it will no longer be a "controversial" topic in dermatology, it will just be accepted as fact.

The only question is: How many more people have to suffer before that happens?

12:06. Final Thoughts on the Future of Topical Steroid Withdrawal (TSW)

Will Topical Steroid Withdrawal (TSW) be recognised as a real medical condition? Yes, but it will take time.

How long will it take? That depends on how much pressure is applied from patients, researchers, and the media.

What can be done to speed it up? People need to speak out louder, share their stories, and demand change.

The fight for Topical Steroid Withdrawal (TSW) recognition is not just about our own suffering, it's about stopping future generations from going through the same thing. Because if things stay the way they are now, more children, more adults, and more families will be destroyed by a condition that should never have existed in the first place.

The future of Topical Steroid Withdrawal (TSW) recognition depends on us.

And we can't afford to stay silent.

Chapter 13. Expert Insights & Scientific Findings on Topical Steroid Withdrawal

While my journey through Topical Steroid Withdrawal (TSW) is deeply personal, it is not unique. Thousands of individuals worldwide have experienced similar patterns of steroid dependence, worsening skin conditions, and severe withdrawal symptoms. Although TSW remains controversial within mainstream dermatology, some experts and medical research have acknowledged its existence and impact.

Expert Opinions on TSW

Dr. Marvin Rapaport, MD, a dermatologist specialising in TSW, has publicly spoken out about the dangers of long-term steroid use. He states:

"Topical steroids are a dangerous treatment for long-term use. What we are seeing with patients suffering from Red Skin Syndrome is not eczema, it is steroid addiction." (Source: The Red Skin Syndrome, Archives of Dermatology)

The National Eczema Association (NEA) has also recognised the potential dangers of long-term steroid use. On their official website, they acknowledge that:

"TSW is a potential side effect of long-term topical steroid use, leading to severe skin inflammation, redness,

and burning sensations after discontinuation."
(Source: National Eczema Association)

Research Supporting TSW as a Medical Condition

Scientific studies have also examined the effects of prolonged topical steroid use. A 2018 study published in The Journal of Dermatology found that long-term use of topical steroids can lead to skin atrophy, increased inflammation upon withdrawal, and potential systemic effects, raising concerns about their prolonged application.

While more research is needed, these studies and expert opinions validate what many patients have experienced firsthand. Despite this, many dermatologists continue to prescribe steroids without fully informing patients of the potential risks.

Further Reading & Resources

For readers who wish to explore more about TSW, the following resources provide additional research, expert insights, and community support:

1, National Eczema Association (NEA) - Topical Steroid Withdrawal
https://nationaleczema.org/topical-steroid-withdrawal

2, Dr. Marvin Rapaport's Research on Red Skin Syndrome
https://itsan.org/resources/research/

3, PubMed Central - Medical Studies on Steroid

Dependence
https://www.ncbi.nlm.nih.gov/pmc/

 The goal of this chapter is not to provide medical advice but to encourage awareness, discussion, and further research. If you are experiencing skin issues or considering changes to your treatment plan, always consult a licensed healthcare provider.

Chapter 14. Speak Out

Chapter 14:01 - Why More People Need to Speak Out

For years, Topical Steroid Withdrawal (TSW) sufferers have been silenced, not just by doctors but by fear, shame, and exhaustion.

People going through one of the most excruciating conditions imaginable are often too mentally and physically drained to advocate for themselves. They are dismissed, ignored, and gaslit by medical professionals.

And when they do speak up? They are told they are "just having a bad eczema flare."

This cycle of denial and suffering has continued for too long. If real change is ever going to happen, more people need to speak out.

But why don't they? And how can we change that?

14:02. Why So Many Topical Steroid Withdrawal (TSW) Survivors Stay Silent

Most people who have gone through the nightmare of Topical Steroid Withdrawal (TSW) should be the loudest voices in the fight for recognition. But instead, many of them disappear once they've healed.

1. The Trauma Is Too Deep

Topical Steroid Withdrawal (TSW) is not just a skin condition, it's a complete breakdown of the body and mind.

It causes isolation, depression, financial ruin, relationship breakdowns, and PTSD.

By the time people recover, they want to put it behind them and move on with their lives.

For many, revisiting their experience feels like reliving the worst time of their lives. They don't want to keep talking about it, they want to forget it ever happened.

2. The Medical System Makes People Feel Crazy

Imagine suffering for years, only to be told by a doctor that what you're going through doesn't exist.

Many people are left questioning their own sanity.

"What if the doctors are right? What if I was just mismanaging my eczema?"

This gaslighting effect leaves people feeling too doubtful and insecure to fight back.

The result? Thousands of Topical Steroid Withdrawal (TSW) sufferers remain silent, believing their pain was an isolated case rather than part of a much bigger problem.

3. Fear of Judgment & Backlash

The moment someone speaks out against the medical

293

system, they face backlash.

Some doctors flat-out refuse to believe Topical Steroid Withdrawal (TSW) is real and will label patients as "non-compliant" or "steroid-phobic."

Even family and friends often don't understand, making sufferers feel even more alone.

Nobody wants to be seen as a conspiracy theorist or a troublemaker, so many choose to stay quiet rather than face criticism.

4. They Don't Want to Scare Others

Topical Steroid Withdrawal (TSW) is terrifying.

Some people don't want to share their stories because they fear it will cause others to panic.

They don't want parents to refuse steroids for their children out of fear, even if steroids work in the short term.

But staying silent only allows more people to suffer in ignorance.

14:03. Why Speaking Out Matters

If Topical Steroid Withdrawal (TSW) is ever going to be recognised as a real medical condition, we need voices.

The more people who speak up, the harder it becomes for doctors to deny. The more stories that are shared, the more sufferers will realise they are not alone. The more awareness that spreads, the more pressure will be put on the medical system to change.

If you're someone who has gone through Topical Steroid Withdrawal (TSW) and come out the other side, you might be wondering: "What can I do to help?"

1. Share Your Story - Even If It's Just Once

You don't have to constantly advocate or become a spokesperson. But sharing your experience just once, whether it's online, in a support group, or in a conversation with a friend, can help someone realise they're not alone.

Ways to Share Your Story:

Social media (Instagram, Facebook, YouTube, TikTok)

Support groups (ITSAN, Reddit, Facebook groups)

Podcasts, blogs, or articles

Talking to friends and family

Every single voice adds to the collective push for change.

2. Report Your Experience to Medical Authorities

Even though the medical system is slow to listen, filing official reports can add up over time.

Report adverse effects of steroids to drug regulatory agencies in your country (such as the FDA in the U.S. or the MHRA in the U.K.).

Tell your dermatologist about your Topical Steroid Withdrawal (TSW) experience, even if they don't believe you, at least it forces them to hear another case.

Participate in any Topical Steroid Withdrawal (TSW) research studies if available, data is what will ultimately force the medical world to accept Topical Steroid Withdrawal (TSW) as real.

3. Support Others Still Going Through It

Even if you don't want to publicly share your own story, helping others privately can make a massive difference.

Check in on people going through Topical Steroid Withdrawal (TSW).

Offer emotional support.

Help them find information and resources.

If recovered Topical Steroid Withdrawal (TSW) sufferers supported new sufferers, the journey would feel less isolating.

4. Demand Change in Dermatology

Ask doctors why they aren't acknowledging Topical Steroid Withdrawal (TSW).

Push for more research.

Encourage people to question long-term steroid use.

The more people demand answers, the harder it becomes for the medical system to ignore the truth.

14:04. Final Thoughts - The Power of Speaking Out

Topical Steroid Withdrawal (TSW) is real. It is happening to thousands of people worldwide. And it is being ignored by those who should be helping us.

But silence is what keeps it hidden.

If every person who has suffered through Topical Steroid Withdrawal (TSW) spoke out, Doctors would be forced to listen.

Medical textbooks would have to be updated.

Fewer people would have to go through this hell without warning.

The future of Topical Steroid Withdrawal (TSW) depends on us. So, whether you're in the middle of withdrawal, fully healed, or just beginning to understand what's happening.

Your voice matters.

Because until the truth is undeniable, the suffering will continue.

Conclusion: How I Plan to Share My Story & What Comes Next

How I Plan to Spread Awareness

- Sharing My Journey Online - I'll continue documenting my recovery through my website (theeczemadeception.com), social media, and Topical Steroid Withdrawal (TSW) support groups, providing updates, advice, and solidarity for those still in the trenches.

- Speaking Out Publicly - If given the chance, I want to talk about Topical Steroid Withdrawal (TSW) on podcasts, in interviews, and even at medical conferences. It's time dermatologists face the people they've ignored.

- Encouraging Others to Speak Up - Every survivor who shares their story adds to the movement. The more voices we have, the harder we are to silence.

- Fighting for Change in Dermatology - No one should have to go through Topical Steroid Withdrawal (TSW) just because they weren't warned about the risks. I want to push for better education and alternatives in dermatology.

- Helping Just One Person Avoid This Hell - If even one person reads this book and chooses a different path before it's too late, then everything I've been through will have been worth it.

But I can't do this alone.

What You Can Do

Share this book. If this story resonated with you, help spread the word. The more people who learn about Topical Steroid Withdrawal (TSW), the faster we can force change.

Tell your story. If you've been through this, don't stay silent. Whether it's in a private group or publicly, your experience matters.

Challenge your doctors. Ask questions. Demand answers. Don't let them brush you off with another prescription.

Support others in the Topical Steroid Withdrawal (TSW) community. This journey is hell, but no one should have to go through it alone. Encourage, listen, and remind others that healing is possible.

Final Thoughts

If you've made it to the end of this book, I want to say 2 things' Thank you. And You are not alone.

I know how isolating this journey is. I know the frustration of going from doctor to doctor, hoping for answers, only to be handed another prescription that makes things worse. I know the exhaustion of waking up every day in pain, the despair of feeling like your body has turned against you, and the fear that this will never end.

But here's what I also know: Healing is possible.

The truth about Topical Steroid Withdrawal (TSW) is buried beneath years of misdiagnosis, misinformation, and medical gas lighting. I had to fight for every piece of knowledge, every small improvement, and every inch of progress. And while my story has been one of pain and loss, it's also a story of survival.

For those still searching for answers, I hope this book has given you clarity. For those trapped in the cycle of steroid dependency, I hope it has given you the courage to question your treatment. And for those already going through withdrawal, I hope it has given you the strength to keep going.

Healing from TSW is not quick. It's not easy. It's not linear. But it does happen.

You will have moments where you feel hopeless. You will doubt yourself. You will question if you made the right choice to stop steroids. But trust me, your body is stronger than you think. Your skin is capable of recovering. And one day, you will wake up and realise the worst is behind you.

This book is my story. But it is also the story of thousands of people worldwide, people who have been let down by a system that was meant to help them. The more we speak out, the more awareness we bring, and the closer we get to ensuring that no one else has to go through this unnecessary suffering.

If you take away anything from this book, let it be this:

- **You are not crazy.**
- **You are not broken.**
- **This is not your fault.**
- **You will heal.**

Keep fighting. Keep believing. And most importantly, keep advocating for yourself, because if I've learned anything, it's that the only person who will truly fight for your health is **you.**

Thank you again.

If you found this book helpful, I'd love to hear from you.

Website: www.theeczemadeception.com

Email: theeczemadeception@gmail.com

Printed in Dunstable, United Kingdom

70870306R00170

L'alessiade, Volume 1

Anna Comnena, Rossi

COLLANA

DEGLI

ANTICHI STORICI GRECI

VOLGARIZZATI.

COLLANA

DEGLI

ANTICHI STORICI GRECI

VOLGARIZZATI.

L' ALESSIADE

DI

ANNA COMNENA

PORFIROGENITA CESAREA

TRADOTTA

PER LA PRIMA VOLTA NELLA ITALIANA LINGUA

DA

GIUSEPPE ROSSI

TOMO PRIMO.

MILANO
DALLA STAMPERIA DI PAOLO ANDREA MOLINA
in Contrada dell' Agnello, N. 965

1846.

PROLOGO

———

I. **I**L tempo irreparabilmente passando con sempre vigoroso discorrimento, porta, sconvolge e trascina seco, vincitore d'ogni indugio ed ostacolo, dal nascer loro tutte le cose, e mette in obblio, senza distinzione, così le meno come le più meritevoli di memoria, sospingendole in mortifero gorgo a sommersione; e con volubile ed inconstante varianza (giusta la tragedia (1)) ora dalle tenebre sviluppa le ignote, ed ora avviluppavi le saputе da prima. Se non che la istoria, qual mole d'insuperabile fortezza, gli contrasta, non dirò già arrestandone il precipitoso corso, ma certamente impedendo che molte delle geste avvenute in esso

———

(1) Sofocle – Aiace flag.

ANNA COMNENA.   1